Understanding Architecture Through Drawing

OTHER TITLES FROM E & FN SPON

Design in Architecture
Architecture and the human sciences
G. Broadbent

Design Strategies in Architecture
An approach to the analysis of form
G. Baker

Elements of Architecture
From form to place
P. von Meiss

Emerging Concepts in Urban Space Design
G. Broadbent

Frank Lloyd Wright and Japan
The role of Japan in the shaping of
Frank Lloyd Wright's organic architecture
K. Nute

Le Corbusier
An analysis of form
G. Baker

Le Corbusier – A Study of Creativity
The formative years of Charles Edouard
Jeanneret
G. Baker

The Way We Build Now
Form, scale and technique
A. Orton

Effective Speaking
Communicating in speech
C. Turk

Effective Writing
Improving scientific, technical and business
communication
C. Turk and J. Kirkman

Good Style
Writing for science and technology
J. Kirkman

Writing Successfully in Science
M. O'Connor

Brain Train
R. Palmer and C. Pope

For more information on these and other titles please
contact: The Promotion Department,
E & FN Spon, 2–6 Boundary Row, London SE1 8HN.
Telephone 071 865 0066

Understanding Architecture Through Drawing

BRIAN W. EDWARDS
DEPARTMENT OF ARCHITECTURE, UNIVERSITY OF HUDDERSFIELD, UK

E & FN SPON
An Imprint of Chapman & Hall

London · Glasgow · New York · Tokyo · Melbourne · Madras

**Published by E & FN Spon, an imprint of
Chapman & Hall, 2-6 Boundary Row, London
SE1 8HN**

Chapman & Hall, 2-6 Boundary Row, London
SE1 8HN, UK

Blackie Academic & Professional, Wester
Cleddens Road, Bishopbriggs, Glasgow G64 2NZ,
UK

Chapman & Hall Inc., One Penn Plaza, 41st
Floor, New York NY10119, USA

Chapman & Hall Japan, Thomson Publishing
Japan, Hirakawacho Nemoto Building , 6F,
1-7-11 Hirakawa-cho, Chiyoda-ku, Tokyo 102,
Japan

Chapman & Hall Australia, Thomas Nelson
Australia, 102 Dodds Street, South Melbourne,
Victoria 3205, Australia

Chapman & Hall India, R. Seshadri, 32 Second
Main Road, CIT East, Madras 600 035, India

First edition 1994
© 1994 Brian Edwards

Typeset in Great Britian by Stephen Cary
Printed in Great Britain by The Alden Press,
Oxford

ISBN 0 419 18640 9

A catalogue record for this book is available from
the British Library

Library of Congress Cataloging-in -Publication
data available

Contents

Introduction

The act of drawing is an important starting point for the intellectual process we call 'design'. To be able to draw a chair or a building is a prerequisite for anyone wishing to design such things. Drawing has two functions for the designer – it allows him or her to record and to analyse existing examples, and the sketch provides the medium with which to test the appearance of some imagined object.

Before the advent of photography most architects kept a sketchbook in which they recorded the details of buildings which they could refer to when designing. The fruits of the Grand Tour or more local wanderings consisted of drawn material supported, perhaps, by written information or surveyed dimensions.

The sketchbook provided a form of research and a library of plans and details to crib at a later stage. Because the architect is not necessarily aiming only at documentary representation, the sketches were often searching and analytical. Many of the drawings prepared found their way into later designs. The English architect C. R. Cockerell used pocket-sized sketchbooks and filled them with drawings not only of sites in Italy and Greece, but of cities in Britain. His sketchbooks which survive at the Royal Institute of British Architects (RIBA) show

that a direct link existed between Cockerell's field studies and his commissions as an architect. Later architects such as Alvar Aalto, Le Corbusier and Louis Kahn employed the sketchbook in a similar fashion though to different ends.

Drawings have been used by architects in many different ways. Ranging between the opposite poles of the freehand drawing as a record and as a design tool exist many different applications for the designer. Some architects use the sketch as the main means of communicating a design idea to clients. Such sketches relay the thinking behind a proposal as well as suggesting a tangible form. Other architects use the sketch to analyse townscape and to indicate how their design will fit into the street. Others use the sketch as a method of studying building typology, using the analysis as a way of placing their design into known precedents. However the sketch is employed, the main point is to use the freehand drawing as a design tool, as a method of giving form and expression to one's thoughts. One may finish the design process with a formal perspective, but that end product should not be where sketching begins. Design analysis through the freehand drawing should be at the start of the creative process, not at the end, and preferably before the design commission arrives in the first

1.1 *This sketch (dated 1862) by Richard Norman Shaw of Bidborough in Kent shows his interest in vernacular buildings. It is no surprise to find Shaw designing new buildings in similar spirit at the time. (RIBA Drawings Collection)*

1.2 *This drawing of a new circular tenement built in Glasgow in 1990 highlights the pattern of windows and shows how the stairways have been used to articulate the design. The sketch seeks to explain the basic geometry of the circular tenement. By eliminating all detail the proportions have become clearer, and what is not evident in the sketch has been highlighted in the notes.*

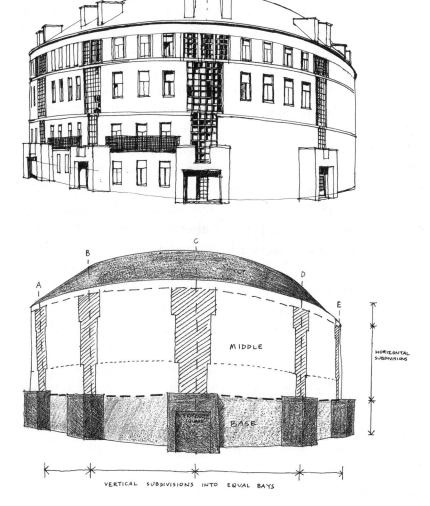

place. The sketchbook is a personal library; it needs to be built up so that it can become a basis for later, undreamt of, designs.

Many architects' drawings leave out a great deal of detail. Whether a sketch is of a design proposal or an existing reality, the element of removal or abstraction is one of the characteristics of such drawings. It is better to capture the essence rather than seek an exhaustive realism. Designers need to know what to leave suggested rather than explicitly recorded. The principles and truth which such drawings seek to communicate can be hidden by too much detail or graphic bombardment. A good drawing is one which leaves room for imaginative interpretation. These principles apply equally to a page in the sketchbook or a drawing prepared to highlight a design proposal.

Sketching and freehand drawing have for too long been seen as the point of entry into painting as against the essential starting point for design. Art colleges have, of course, always maintained a sketchbook tradition among artists and designers alike, but in sixth-form colleges, and even schools of architecture, the sketchbook has been usurped by the computer simulation or verbal description.

What this book seeks to revive is the sketch and analytical drawing as means of understanding form and construction. Only through the study of existing examples – not laboriously drawn but critically examined – can we cultivate a nation of people

1.4 *Glazing details are not always as expressive as here at the Financial Times printing works (designed by Nicholas Grimshaw and Partners) in East London. Notice how the sketch is supplemented by a freehand section.*

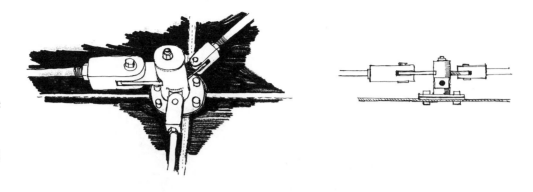

1.5 *The windows of the Pump Room in Bath make an attractive pattern from both the inside and outside. As with much Georgian architecture, elements such as shop fronts and sash windows are framed with margins and mouldings.*

4

1.6 *Charles Rennie Mackintosh possessed a unique vision which embraced not only his freehand drawings and watercolours, but also his designs as an architect. This sketch (dated 1901) by him of the castle at Holy Island in Northumberland is similar in spirit to his more adventurous designs, especially in the three-dimensional treatment of gables. (Glasgow University: Mackintosh Collection)*

sensitive to design and its application to our everyday environment. This willingness to learn from past examples should apply across the board, from an appreciation of townscapes to the design of children's furniture.

Questions of scale are hardly relevant – we live in a designed environment, whether we as consumers are aware of it or not. Every lamp standard and traffic sign has been 'designed', the layout of motorway junctions has been shaped by an engineer with an eye to beauty as well as safety. On a smaller scale, our cutlery and crockery are designed, as are the disposable wrappings at the fast-food restaurant.

The sketchbook allows us to be aware of this reality as long as students are encouraged to explore through drawing. The welcome changes to the national curriculum to enhance the status of design and craft teaching, and the broadening of appeal of courses in architecture, landscape design and town planning, have created an unprecedented interest in the environment and design. To turn this interest into a better-designed world requires the development of graphic and visual skills.

In a sense we are all designers, even if we do not make our living through the medium of design. As designers we modify our immediate environment through changing the décor of our houses, or designing our own clothes, to choosing consumer objects on the basis of how they look as well as how they work. We are sold products and services partly by design – you have only to watch television advertising to realize that our aesthetic sensibilities are being appealed to even when the product being promoted is as unglamorous as double glazing.

Prince Charles has awakened the national consciousness over questions of urban quality and architectural design. He uses the sketchbook as a means of describing and understanding the places he likes. The sketch is employed as a learning tool rather than as mere description.

The untrained eye can learn a great deal through drawing. It teaches an important visual discipline –

1.7 *The drawing of Merriot Church in Somerset by Mackintosh provided the inspiration for the design of the tower of Queen's Cross Church in Glasgow a couple of years later in 1897. (Glasgow University: Mackintosh Collection).*

1.8 This sketch (dated 1991) by the architect Richard Reid sets his design proposals for Gravesend in Kent into the streetscape. This type of exploratory sketch is part of the process most architects employ to test the appearance of their ideas.

an awareness of shape, line and perspective. The sketch also engenders respect for the environment and the designed objects within it. To have sat for an hour and drawn an old panelled door is to create a respect for the object which may discourage the tendency to daub it with graffiti, or to relegate it to firewood. Such doors could be recycled if their qualities or beauty were respected, and the sketch rather than the instantly obtained photograph is the means to this awareness.

It is said that in our modern world we now produce more photographs than bricks. For the first time in history the visual image has become more important than the means of making houses. The lesson concerns the importance of design and appearance in contemporary society. But photographs are not always the most appropriate medium for expressing this visual concern. There are times, and subjects, which lend themselves to

graphic analysis, rather than pictorial description. This book has the aim of reviving the sketchbook tradition, in order to create a visually literate society. The objective of education is to achieve not just literacy and numeracy, but graphic, visual and spatial skills. Our success as an industrial society requires this; and so do we, whether as designers or as individuals.

If this book encourages people – professional designers or otherwise – to explore the environment round about them with sketchbook and pencil (as against camera) in hand, then a useful beginning would have been made. There are always subjects to learn from, whether we choose to live in city, suburb or countryside. This book takes themes based upon everyday experience, and seeks to draw design lessons from them. Once we have learnt the language of drawing and graphic analysis, we are then in a position to engage in the

1.9 At the level of house design, sketches by the architect Sir Basil Spence explore options for the general arrangement of the plan. Spence relates the plan to how the house will look from afar. The design is for Gribloch near Glasgow, built in 1938. (NMRS: Spence Collection)

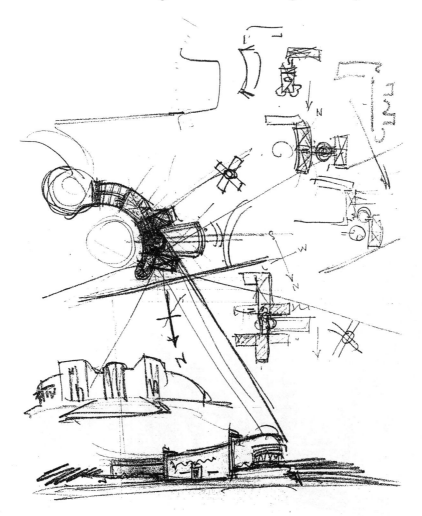

complex business of design. For the first time in history design involves us all and has permeated through to every aspect of our lives. If we ignore the language of design, we will be as disadvantaged as those who finish school without the basic skills of literacy and numeracy. No single book can teach us how to learn through drawing, but it can point us in the right direction and open our eyes to the benefit of good design.

TYPES OF DRAWING

To the architect and urban designer there are three main types of freehand drawing. The first is the elaborate perspective drawing used to communicate design ideas to clients or planning authorities. Increasingly this type of drawing is produced by computer. The second type concerns the production of sketch perspectives and views used to communicate design ideas to specialists such as engin-

eers, and sometimes to help clarify points for the designer's own benefit. This type of drawing can be split into:

- the investigation of an early design;
- exploring methods of construction;
- testing the visual effect of details;
- setting the design in its physical context.

The third type of freehand drawing concerns the exploration of the existing world, its buildings, details and landscapes. The use of drawing in this regard does not just provide a repertoire of forms and designs to use in developing new structures, but helps cultivate a sensitivity towards the existing context in which architects, planners and landscape architects are increasingly required to work.

Of these three broad categories of drawing, this book focuses upon the latter. With a growing awareness of the cultural and aesthetic values of cities, and with the European Community requiring ever higher standards of urban design, those in the environmental professions face new challenges.

The general public, too, is better informed and through local amenity societies and bodies like the National Trust make their views known on an unprecedented scale. The widening of education to embrace design and technology (under the national curriculum reforms of 1990) promises to focus yet more attention upon design in public fields such as architecture. Hence the world of the professions has been opened to challenge by an informed public, with design no longer the monopoly of people with letters after their names.

Before the modern design professions were established, students and practitioners employed the sketchbook as a matter of course. They were not topographical artists but people in search of creative material. The Arts and Crafts architect George Devey studied under John Sell Cotman in Norwich in the 1830s, thereby absorbing not just Cotman's approach to freehand drawing, but a whole collection of details of windmills, barns, country houses, castles and cottages which later proved invaluable to Devey the architect. Similarly, Richard Norman Shaw, Ernest George, John Keppie and, later, Edwin Lutyens continued to use the sketchbook to record the towns and buildings not just of Britain, but of Europe and the Middle East. One can trace the origins of the architectural sketchbook back to the Renaissance, but its blossoming as a creative force in its own right owes much to the 19th century.

The sketchbook is a personal record – a dialogue between artist and subject. The nature of the dialogue determines the quality or use of the finished drawing. By engaging in the subject, the artist, architect or student develops a sensitivity and understanding difficult to obtain by other means. The blind copying of subject is not necessarily useful – a critical stance is required. One may never use the sketch produced of the town or landscape – at least not directly – but, like reading a good book, the insights gained may prove invaluable later on.

The designer needs to be accomplished in the three main areas of drawing mentioned earlier. To be able to render a convincing perspective is an essential skill; to explore the detailing of an unbuilt structure through sketches avoids pitfalls in the final design; and to use freehand drawing to learn from past examples helps the architect or urban designer to give better shape to townscapes of the future. The environmental awareness which is a feature of our post-industrial society has encouraged a return to questions of firmness, commodity and delight. These are the qualities the Arts and Crafts architects sought to discover through their sketchbook investigations. This book seeks to pick up the threads of a drawing tradition, and to use them to teach us lessons about the contemporary city, its buildings and landscapes.

A NOTE ABOUT THE SKETCHES

In this book all of the sketches by the author (i.e. all the drawings not attributed to other artists) were prepared on location. In some instances shading or colour has subsequently been added to enhance the drawing or explain more clearly an aspect of the design. The sketch plans or cross-sections are generally drawn from memory or with the help of town plans or other publications. In some examples the analytical plan was prepared on location on the basis of cognition rather than formal mapping.

Drawings by other designers have been employed to show that their method of sketching influenced how they looked at buildings, and hence how they designed new ones. This is particularly true of Charles Rennie Mackintosh whose sparse lines and large areas of unadorned wall planes lead directly to his modern designs. The drawings by Richard Norman Shaw, Mackintosh and others show also that the same subjects can be viewed in quite different ways, with obvious consequences for their approach to design. This is true not only of famous architects of earlier periods but of practising designers today such as Richard Reid and Arup Associates.

Part One
Guiding Principles

Chapter 2

Why draw?

There is an undisguised air of evangelism running through this book, for it seeks to encourage students of architecture, craft and design to forsake their cameras and learn the art of freehand sketching. Drawing is not only more enjoyable and far more educational, but the end product is more likely to remain a cherished object than would an anonymous slide or photographic print. Drawing an object, building or townscape forces you to engage more directly in the subject than as a mere photographer; the search to record shape, proportion, detail and colour requires greater effort and more skilled observation than that needed to press the shutter of a camera. The discriminatory eye encouraged through sketching has value to the potential designer and tourist alike for it engages the observer in an important dialogue with his or her subject.

Until fairly recently the sketchbook was the accepted accompaniment of all students of architecture or landscape, and of many interested tourists. In many ways Prince Charles maintains this honourable tradition. Before photography became more affordable and part of our visual culture, the sketch remained the means to record and analyse an interesting town, building, or piece of furniture. You have only to look at the sketchbooks of famous architects – from Robert Adam to Charles Rennie Mackintosh – to see how valued was the freehand sketch. Its use was often beyond that of mere record or pretty picture: invariably the sketch was the means of noting down a particular detail or type of composition that could be used when the right design commission came along. For instance, Adam's sketches of the fortifications of the Dalmation coast were transformed in less than a decade into the 18th-century Scottish castles occupying a more northern coastline.

Many students of architecture and design spend a great deal of time and money making photographs and rather less on sketching. They could, of course, buy postcards or tourist guides, which often contain better and more accurate pictures at only a fraction of the cost, thereby concentrating their efforts instead on the harder but more valuable process of drawing. What the sketchbook provides is a means of delving deeper into the subject than merely recording it, in order to begin to understand why and how the scene was shaped. The main barrier to using the sketchbook in this way appears to be the lack of basic graphic skills, together with the hectic pace of modern life. As with all endeavours of value, you have to practise a great deal to cultivate the craft of freehand drawing, in order to fulfil the potential offered by the sketchbook.

The drawing skills are outlined in this book under simple headings such as shade, line weight, composition and rules of perspective. As with learning to play a musical instrument, you have to spend time practising and training eye-to-hand co-ordination The rules of drawing are, like the rules of grammar or numeracy, based upon a language we all share and understand. By combining elements of the 'craft of drawing' with 'graphic rules', you will quickly develop a technique suitable to your particular needs – whether as a student of architecture, design or landscape, or simply as an inquisitive tourist on holiday abroad.

The process of sketching is not presented in these pages as an end in itself, but as a means of raising the student's awareness of design by cultivating careful, well-directed skills of observation. The sketch is both a record and a statement of visual inquiry. The act of drawing from life, be it of a town or a building, is to engage the artist in the subject in a unique and rewarding fashion. If the sketch is undertaken in the spirit of formal investigation, then the results can be considerable in terms of the development of personal design skills. The linear progression from sketchbook analysis to design proposal is one which many architects have experienced. The detailed study of a subject through the freehand drawing leads naturally to creative design by opening up different possibilities. Analysing existing buildings through the pages of the sketchbook provides a useful spring-

2.1 *This elegant sketch (of 1880) by William Lethaby of the High Street, Exeter, displays a concern for construction and structural expression. (RIBA Drawings Collection)*

2.2 *Richard Reid's analytical drawings (of 1990) of farm buildings led, at least indirectly, to the design of his visitor centre at Chartwell for the National Trust.*

tithe Barn, Upper Heyford, Oxfordshire c 1400

brick granary c. 1810, at Tytherington Wiltshire

Great Coxwell Barn, Oxfordshire mid 13ᵗʰc – one of finest surviving medieval barns in England.

interior of aisled barn

early 16ᵗʰc barn Grange Farm, Basing, Hampshire

Oast houses, farm near Edenbridge, Kent. – my central structure is the cooling area.

2.3 *The exploration of modern architecture can be as rewarding as that of historic buildings. This swimming pool in Sheringham, Norfolk, by architects Alsop and Lyall, makes expressive use of exposed beams, guttering and angled glazing. Shadows on the sketch help bring out the structural arrangements.*

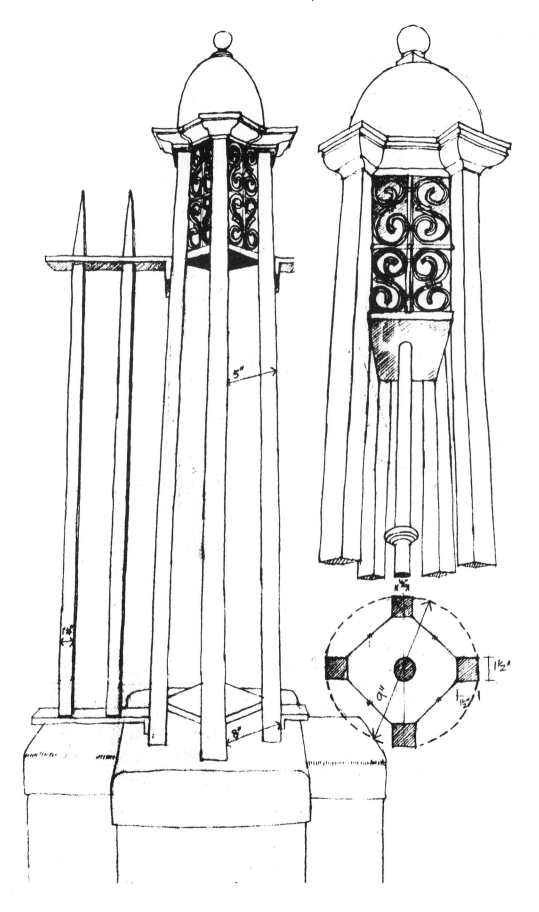

2.4 Decorative railings can be taxing to draw but the effort is worth while if it leads to the preservation of attractive features. This sketch was prepared as a measured survey prior to re-erection at the Royal Victoria Hospital, Newcastle upon Tyne.

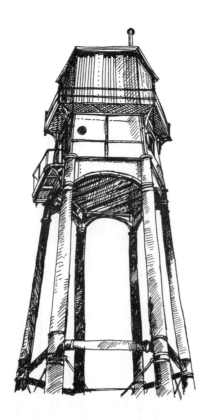

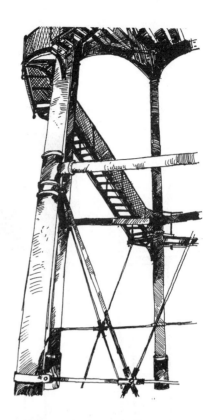

2.5 *The 19th-century lighthouse at Dovercourt in Essex has an undisguised steel frame and expressive bracing. The subject lends itself to pen and ink drawing with shading used to enhance the spacing of the columns and beams.*

2.6 *At a more detailed level the steelwork of the lighthouse at Dovercourt continues to give expression to how the structure is supported and braced against the coastal winds.*

board for progressing into design. The precedents explored are of value in themselves, but, more importantly, the formal, spatial and decorative language employed in examples which have been sketched may prove applicable to the design of new buildings.

To take advantage of the progression from freehand drawing to creative design, the artist must approach the subject in a considered fashion. The outline is important and so are the proportions, and often a relationship exists between the building in plan and how it works in section and elevation. As we tend to draw the outsides of buildings, the potential designer should not focus upon the façades at the expense of the often critical relationship between elevation and plan. These 'invisible' relationships may be the most instructive when drawing certain buildings, and provide a source of ideas for the designer.

A good sketch is not necessarily a faithful likeness; it may in a pedagogic sense be better to analyse and decipher the subject. Sketches which consist of probings around specific themes may prove particularly useful to designers since they provide fruitful avenues for further exploration.

Charles Rennie Mackintosh was a particular master of this type of sketch and drawings from his Italian Tour of 1891 demonstrate a concern for form and decoration which are obvious precursors of his later designs. In his sketchbook drawings Mackintosh explores the volumetric nature of Italian churches, the simple almost abstract forms of farmhouses, and the black and white decoration of Romanesque chapels. These images and the facility Mackintosh developed for representing them find expression, either directly or indirectly, in his later designs for schools and houses. Similar sketchbook studies of Celtic art and architecture, and of wild flowers sketched whilst living in Suffolk, proved a parallel path into creative design for Mackintosh.

The architect Richard Reid uses the sketchbook in a similar fashion today. His studies of oasthouses in Kent were the inspiration for his design for a National Trust visitor centre at Chartwell. The freehand drawings provided a source of references which Reid selectively exploited for his new design. The skill Reid demonstrates in his sketching has enriched his experience as a modern designer. In fact in the work of Reid and Mackintosh it is

Why draw?

2.7 *This sketch made at a street café in Andraixt in Majorca is drawn in pencil on smooth cartridge paper. The shading is intended to reflect the patina of ageing on old rendered façades.*

2.8 *Drawn with a black felt pen, these buoys in Harwich harbour make an attractive assembly of strange shapes. Shadow has been employed to highlight the patterns and to distinguish between the buoyancy chambers and the protective grilles around the warning lights.*

17

difficult to draw a rigid line between the creative artist and the creative designer.

There is a further advantage for the designer in developing sketchbook skills. The graphic facility cultivated in freehand drawing aids the representation of design proposals. The means of recording an existing subject are much the same as those employed in depicting an unbuilt vision of the future. The graphic language is the same whether the building exists in reality or simply in one's imagination: the use of line and shadow, of weighted and feint lines, of exaggerated silhouette, and so on, are employed with equal meaning. The skills needed for drawing, once learnt, are far speedier

2.9 *This pencil drawing of courtyard planting in Palma in Majorca employs shading to throw the giant palm leaves forward. The different scales and sizes of foliage makes planting the dominant element in this domestic space.*

and more responsive than those required for model making or computer graphics. Drawing also conveys a sense of spirit, of creative passion, which other forms of representation often lack.

Just as the sketchbook can be used to dissect graphically an existing building, the technique of unravelling and abstracting different architectural features can be employed in the reverse – to represent the different elements of a design proposal. The explanation of form, structure and decoration can help in the development of design especially where complex matters of building services and space management are involved. A line of continuity therefore links the analysis of existing buildings

2.10 *Watercolour expresses the cool, smooth abstract qualities of this attractive corner building in San Felice Circeo in Italy.*

2.11 This sequence of four comparisons of sketches and photographs of central Glasgow shows the benefits of freehand drawing. In each case unnecessary information has been edited out in order to focus upon the architectural qualities. Whilst the photographs include all the detail, the sketches interpret their subject and highlight specific topics relevant to the designer.

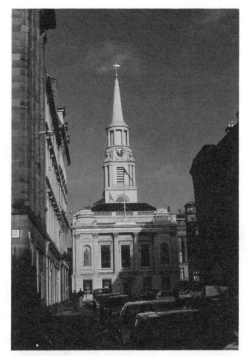

to the development of new ones, with a similar range of drawing techniques being employed. This is one of the lessons that may be learnt by studying the drawings of architects of the calibre of Mackintosh.

MATERIALS

The artist of today has never been so fortunate with regard to drawing equipment. Modern water-proof felt pens, clutch pencils and a wide range of drawing papers mean that every situation, type of subject and sketching style is catered for. The decision nowadays tends to be what to leave behind, since the range of materials is so wide and their reliability so good.

Generally speaking, smooth cartridge sketch-books (of the Daler type) are best for line work in pen; coarser paper for line work in pencil; and

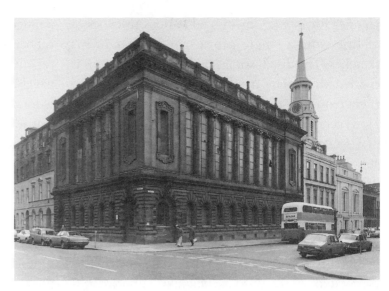

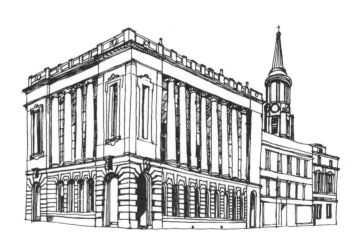

strong watercolour paper for paints or colour markers. When choosing sketchbook paper, you should have already decided upon your sketching medium. Ideally, of course, you will have prepared for working in different materials and have corresponding sketchbooks to suit.

I prefer to use modern felt-tipped pens (such as a waterproof Pilot or Staedtler) with smooth, fairly thin paper (such as a Daler 3404 sketchbook).

Drawing pens with india ink tend to clog up or flow too slowly for my style of drawing. Alternatively, you can use a steel-nibbed pen (such as a post office nib) which is simply pushed into a pen holder and dipped as required into a pot of ink. The great advantage of old-fashioned steel nibs is that the thickness of line varies with the pressure exerted, so that sketches have a lot more character and points of emphasis. The architect and town planner Raymond Unwin used various thicknesses of line from a single nib to good effect in his sketches. The disadvantage of the open steel nibs is the length of time it takes for the ink to dry and their tendency to cast ink blots in all directions. However, with patience, good sunlight and a box of tissues, the problems can be overcome, and should you make an ink blot, this can either be worked into the drawing, or left to dry and scraped away with a sharp blade and ink rubber.

I try to encourage my students not to become weighed down with too many drawing materials – it is best to travel light and learn to improvise. It is no good for the artist to become like a photographer impeded by an assortment of lenses and light meters. All you really need is an A4 or A5 sketchbook, one or two pens or pencils and a good rubber.

The size of sketchbook depends upon the type of drawing you intend to do, and the medium you are working with. Large-format sketchbooks (A3–A2 in size) suit pastel drawing or watercolours rather than line drawing. As a rule, the finer the line, the smaller the sketchbook required. If you wish to mix line with paint, then the effect is rather more of a painting than of a drawing, and consequently a large format is generally preferred.

I tend not to use sketching stools these days, partly because pavements are so busy, and partly because stools are rather cumbersome. You can, however, buy sketching stools with pockets for carrying pens, etc., and with a large flap for holding an A4 sketchbook, but I still prefer to find a café to sit outside. Often the places you wish to draw are the very spots where people want to sit and enjoy the view, and hence seats will have been provided by a friendly town council. In old towns there are generally lots of steps and walls to sit upon, and inside cathedrals you will find comfortable pews or quiet cloisters with stone benches in which to enjoy a couple of hours of sketching. The one advantage of the sketching stool, however, is that you can choose the exact viewpoint for the drawing, and this can be important for certain subjects.

If you are drawing in pencil make sure you have a range of pencils of varying softness (6B–B), a soft rubber, fixative and a sharpener. Some people prefer clutch pencils, but many others prefer the weight and feel of the traditional pencil for field work. Pencil is a good starting point for people learning to draw since corrections are easily made and the graphite or lead pencil has a 'graininess' suitable for many building subjects. Pencil also lends itself to depicting shade, light and shadow and this may be important in canyon-like street scenes. Pencil drawings have one other advantage: they can be photocopied to highlight or darken the tentative lines of a timid artist. Indeed, modern photocopiers can be a useful adjunct: not only can they encourage confidence in beginners, but in addition, several copies of a drawing may be taken (if, for instance, the sketch is the beginning for further analysis or the starting point for other artistic endeavours), while the original drawing is preserved.

Armed with a soft rubber, drawing with graphite pencil is the best way to start freehand sketching, being flexible, responsive and easily alterable. Whether your sketches are spontaneous and primitive, or intricate and spatially accurate compositions reflecting a trained eye, pencil will probably serve your needs well. It should be remembered, however, that graphite pencils quickly smudge, especially if you are using a coarse drawing paper. It is imperative, therefore, that you spray lightly and frequently with fixative. Having mastered the technique of pencil drawing, the artist can then graduate to sketching in charcoal, pen and ink, or using colour washes.

Watercolour washes can be used to support pen or pencil drawings in order to give the appearance of three-dimensional form. Many people like to use grey wash along with line work to produce rather classical sketches of the type favoured in the 18th century. You can mix your own grey wash, or do as I prefer and make a grey by blending cobalt blue with sepia. The resulting wash is less 'dead' than a grey watercolour straight from the tube since hints of blue and brown appear as the wash dries. Sometimes a pre-mixed wash can be employed, especially if the sketch has to be produced in a hurry, but often the wash varies in density to the detriment of the finished drawing.

Watercolour can, of course, be employed to produce illustration in its own right. For watercolour sketches use a box of 12 colours which come with a mixing box (Windsor and Newton, for instance) and two or three sable brushes. Try to use largish brushes to avoid the sketches becoming overworked, and if you like you can take a crayon or candle to experiment with wax relief to produce the sort of lively architectural sketches made famous by John Piper. For mood and character, dark-toned watercolour sketches can hardly be bettered, but you will find paint a difficult medium for analytical drawing.

Coloured felt pens can be difficult to master since their hues are often rather strong and do not mix well together. But some subjects lend themselves to these pens (especially modern architectur-al subjects and industrial or automobile design). By mixing the bright, almost luminous quality of felt pens with more neutral paints or pencil lines, the sketch can assume a sparkle or resonance appropriate to certain subjects. Felt pens and magic markers are difficult to master but they have a place in both the modern design studio and amongst the sketching tools of an adventurous street artist.

Although I was taught never to use a ruler when sketching, I do not now subscribe to this view. So many of our landscapes and buildings are rectilinear in nature that the use of a ruler to help establish the basic outline and structure can no longer be considered a lazy short cut. The straight-edge is, however, no substitute for the trained eye. If the sketch is as much learning process as end product, the ruler may help the latter but does not assist the former. Hence use the straight-edge if you will, but do not expect to learn much from the assistance it gives.

Chapter 3

Choosing the subject

It is no good dashing off a sketch on your first visit to a new city or to an interesting building. Such hurried sketches are generally poorly composed or suffer from having the light in the wrong direction. It is worth taking your time and planning the drawing carefully. The chief points to consider are:

- what drawing materials are best for the sketch in question;
- from where should you draw;
- what time of day is best for the sketch, bearing in mind the angle of light, especially sunlight;
- what position is best to bring out the character of the subject and produce an attractive composition?

Taking the first point about materials, you will probably find that certain subjects suit a particular sketching medium. For example, a highly decorative subject such as the west front of a cathedral would suit a line drawing in pen and ink, perhaps with depth being created by a sepia or grey wash to indicate shadows. The interior of the cathedral, on the other hand, may suit a charcoal drawing since the darkness and solidity of the columns, vaulting and arches could be brought out in thick grainy lines and smudged tones. An Italian hill town may

be best rendered in watercolour as this may suit the delineation of the pink, brown and orange walls and roofs. A classical terrace by John Nash may look its best in pencil with a soft wash of cream added. A modern 'high tech' building such as the Lloyds Insurance offices in London or the Pompidou Centre in Paris could be tackled in pen and wash with brightly coloured felt pens being used to pick out the externally placed lifts and services. Whatever materials are employed, the artist should try to establish a relationship between the qualities of the subject and the drawing medium.

Deciding where you should sit to draw on location raises both aesthetic and practical issues. You will often find that your subject is near the town centre and hence very busy, or so frequented by tourists that you can hardly obtain an unobstructed view. Hence you will need to plan your sketch to fit in with siesta times (if on the Continent), or to take place in the early morning or late evening if in the city centre. Sometimes you can find a quiet corner even in the busiest town, but often it will be dirty or the odours will be inconducive to good sketching. If you have a sketching stool then your options may be greatly increased, but try to avoid positions where crowds of curious children can peer over your shoulder (and maybe steal your spare pencils). If you have to find public seats, low walls or steps to sit upon, then planning in advance is doubly necessary. You might well find that the best angles for drawing are also those preferred by tourists, and sometimes the best sketching position places you in the shade or in a draughty corner. Drawing a Mediterranean town in the warm sun-shine of a June afternoon is a rare pleasure, and with good planning you may be able to find a street café where for the price of a cup of coffee you will have an uninterrupted hour for drawing.

You are likely to produce a better sketch if you are warm and have a little privacy. Besides crowds, try to avoid sitting in areas full of traffic fumes since this is not only unhealthy, but the dust and dirt will mark your paper and discolour your washes. Traffic is usually unavoidable, but if you study which way the breeze is blowing, you may be able to find an area less troubled by fumes even in a congested city like Rome or Athens. Often it is only a case of deciding which side of a square or street to sit in order to avoid the traffic fumes and

RHYME

3.1 *A drawing of this complexity can only be undertaken with the façades bathed in sunlight. The level of detail and degree of patterning requires bright, preferably diagonal, light to pick out the extraordinary detail. Known as Templeton's Factory and situated in Glasgow's east end, this handsome Victorian building looks across an exten-sive park.*

3.2 *This drawing of Edinburgh Castle seeks to express the aggregation of parts which make up complex buildings. It also tries to communicate the fact that it is built of stone and sits upon a stone clifftop.*

enjoy the sunshine on yourself and on the subject.

The angle of light and particularly sunlight can make the difference between a good and a bad sketch, and hence affect your ability to learn from the process of drawing. You will generally need the sunshine to be on your subject and preferably at an angle rather than straight on. This brings out any sculptural modelling or surface relief, allowing the artist to understand the nuances of the building or the intentions of its designer. Certainly it is useful to highlight or exaggerate effects of light, especially in older buildings where time has worn away the sharpness of the detail. Try to avoid having the source of light behind the subject, unless you are deliberately attempting to draw its silhouette. Cathedrals lend themselves to dramatic silhouette and it is quite permissible to exaggerate the effects of light on the city skyline. The Manhattan skyline or a castle such as that at Edinburgh, perched on a dramatic hilltop, lend themselves to silhouette drawing, but the sketch may benefit from having detail shown at ground level drawn as open line rather than dark craggy shapes. Such drawings can tell us about the role of the 'monuments' in the city and their prominent positions in the skyline. The role of lesser buildings and foreground detail is merely supportive – a point not always recognized by modern architects or town planners.

Sunlight also casts shadows, which can provide tonal relief to a line drawing. A collection of lines can appear rather abstract, while shadow or shading gives the drawing a feeling of solidity and three-dimensional form. Shadows can also give an indication of buildings behind or to one side of the artist, but not in his or her field of view. It is worth bearing this in mind if you are drawing in the street or in a square. Shadows give an indication, too, of deep canyon-like streets as against open suburban

3.3 *The complicated façade of the Pompidou Centre in Paris is set against a dark sky to draw attention to the building's expressive silhouette. The exposed ducting and pipework make an attractive substitute for columns and walls.*

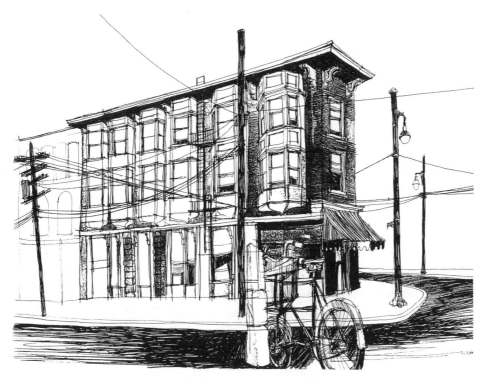

3.4 *Street scenes like this are best attempted when the traffic has died down. This 19th-century 'flat iron' building in Vancouver shares a busy road junction with lamp-posts, telegraph wires and the occasional delivery bicycle.*

3.5 *This drawing of the swimming pool by Alsop and Lyall in Sheringham, Norfolk, was drawn from inside a car in order to provide shelter, and privacy, and the best angle for the sketch.*

roads. Sketching should aim at capturing the character of places, and the play of sunlight with its consequent casting of shadows is part of the visual repertoire to be exploited.

The depth of shadow is important. Northern subjects illuminated with soft light suit the faintest of shadows, but a southern Baroque church or Moorish temple is best rendered in deep shadow. It has been suggested that the extent of modelling of a building's façade directly reflects the anticipated level of sunlight, a south- or west-facing frontage being designed with plenty of deep relief whilst a north-facing façade has a more subdued quality. These subtleties are often only made manifest to the observer through the act of drawing.

One of the professional tricks of the contemporary architect is to draw a bland office façade with plenty of deep shadows, thereby suggesting a building of greater visual richness than the one to be finally built. In this way the designer may 'persuade' a planning committee or amenity society to accept the proposals. The normal method of show-

ing shadows is to assume a sun at 45° over your left shoulder – hence the window sills and eaves can then be picked out with a dark-blue or even black shadow. Designers have long realized that they can enhance the appearance of their proposals by using shadows based upon an abstract and decidedly flexible view of reality. In many ways the artist drawing a street scene or building can adopt this device and in the process make a dull northern scene look quite lively. Even if the sun is not shining, the assumption that it can enhances a subject and makes its visual qualities more accessible to you as artist, and to those who look at your sketch.

Choosing the position to draw from is also largely an aesthetic matter. The relationship between the parts of a sketch is important and you should seek to achieve a measure of harmony or balance in the drawing. The elements to consider are those features in shadow and those picked out by the sun, those which can be rendered in line as against tone, and the parts in elevation as against perspective. All these factors dictate where you choose to sit, what time of day you select to draw, and what materials you employ.

Taking time to consider these elements saves you from frustrations later when the drawing does not work out in spite of all your efforts. The sketch is really a piece of design, and hence a great deal of thought and planning is required. It is unusual that you can race into a drawing and be pleased with the results, or feel you have learnt from the experience.

Sketching should be both enjoyable and educational; and both may be helped by a little contemplative peace. As such you are likely to be happier in a quiet leafy courtyard than a busy high street, and in the side chapel of a cathedral as against the nave.

Search out quiet corners and try to have a wall behind you if strangers looking over your shoulder make you feel uneasy. One other tip about selecting your spot for sketching: choose somewhere which feels safe (street crime is unfortunately on the increase in most European cities) and keep an eye on your wallet or handbag.

Part Two
Techniques

Chapter 4

Perspective

An understanding of perspective is essential for both the full appreciation of the aesthetic quality of towns and the ability to draw them. Many cities, especially those based upon classical principles of town planning, exploit perspective in their arrangement of streets and squares, and if you do not understand the principles of perspective, you can hardly be expected to draw them adequately. Likewise, many building interiors are so arranged that a grasp of perspective is essential not only if you are going to attempt to sketch them, but in order to understand their spatial qualities.

Designers are able to visualize the volumetric arrangement of their buildings simply by conceiving them in terms of true perspective. Sir Christopher Wren was one of the first architects to admit that an understanding of perspective was vital for the design of a building. Perspective allows the architect or designer to anticipate the relationship of the parts of the design without making a model or drawing a line. As we see towns in terms of the routes and streets we take, and buildings in terms of room and corridors, a grasp of linear perspective is a fundamental starting point for spatial comprehension.

The discovery of true perspective was one of the high points of Renaissance art. A handful of artists working in Florence in the 15th century stumbled upon the rules of perspective, and quickly exploited it in their paintings. Soon after it was adopted by architects, who arranged their buildings and squares with mathematical precision. The resulting environment seems almost to have the expression of perspective as the central point of the design. Proportional harmony and repeating bay sizes lent themselves to presentation through perspective either in the form of paintings or architectural sketches. Later, in the Baroque period, town planning exploited perspective by creating long vistas of streets or tree-lined avenues ending almost at infinity or terminating with a public building. Without the discovery of geometrically correct perspective, grand designs such as Versailles or the Nash terraces in London would have been unthinkable.

To draw such towns one must understand perspective, but sketching in the street does not require the production of drawing-board perspectives based upon rotating picture planes and mathematical precision. In fact, these elaborate perspective drawings can become so complicated that they discourage you from drawing on location at all. It is a case of the science of perspective becoming an obstacle to learning the simple principles of perspective.

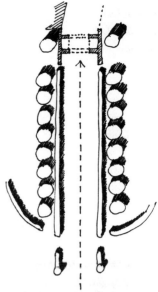

4.1 *The axis of this garden in Siena exploits single-point perspective. The garden walk is terminated at one end by a gateway and at the other by a formal flower bed.*

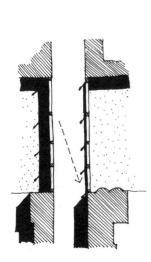

4.2 *An understanding of perspective allows complex subjects such as this double bow-fronted Georgian house in Ayr to be drawn with confidence. Notice how windows in the distance are rendered as mere vertical lines, and the use of hatching focuses the eye on the critical parts of the design.*

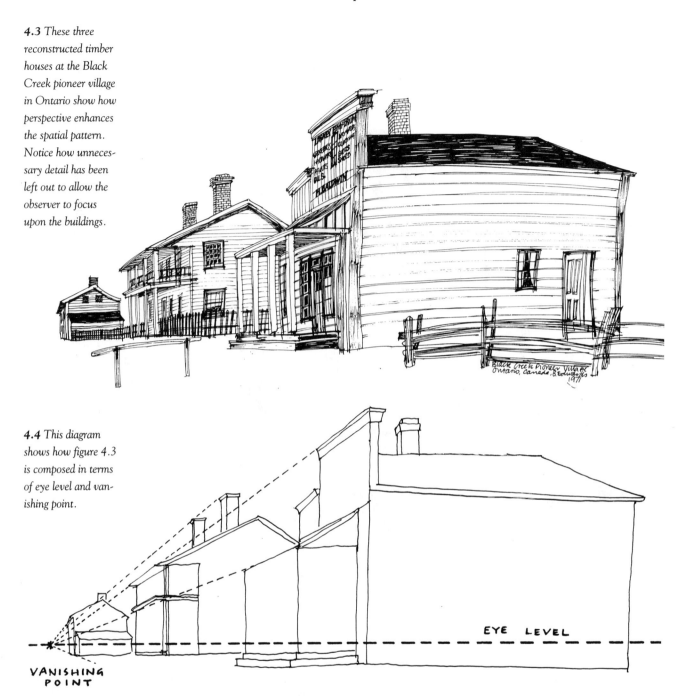

4.3 *These three reconstructed timber houses at the Black Creek pioneer village in Ontario show how perspective enhances the spatial pattern. Notice how unnecessary detail has been left out to allow the observer to focus upon the buildings.*

4.4 *This diagram shows how figure 4.3 is composed in terms of eye level and vanishing point.*

EYE LEVEL

VANISHING POINT

Indeed, for most subjects it is only necessary to understand the basic rules of perspective – that parallel lines focus upon vanishing points which are spaced along your eye level. This simple principle applies irrespective of the angles of the object (in plan) or changes in the level of the ground. Of course, if there are slopes or ramps to draw, these are not level and hence have their own vanishing point above or below those for horizontal lines, depending upon whether the slope or ramp is angled up or down.

Single-point perspective is the easiest to employ in the field and the most useful for townscape and landscape drawing. It focuses attention upon the space rather than the object, and for this reason is a great aid when drawing squares, streets and interiors. The buildings or walls at right angles to the observer are simply elevations drawn without angle to left or right. Single-point perspective suits the sketching of towns laid out on axial planning principles, or interiors with parallel corridors and plenty of right-angled spaces. Hence it is very useful for

4.5 *The widely set vanishing points of this sketch of Charles Rennie Mackintosh's Hill House near Glasgow allow the rambling composition to be included on a single sheet.*

4.6 *Two-point perspective focuses attention upon objects in space rather than on the space around buildings. Here in Blythswood Square in central Glasgow the composition retains its original arrangement.*

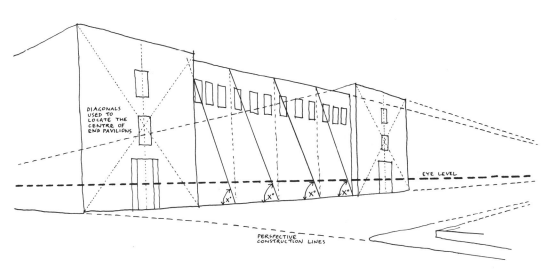

4.7 *The use of diagonals and repeating bays allows the complex façade of Blythswood Square to be set down fairly accurately. The left- and right-hand vanishing points are off the page. Notice how the angle X° remains the same for the house's subdivisions.*

drawing classical compositions, whether in terms of buildings or whole towns. Since the streets are normally straight and often have terminating features at the vanishing point, perspective allows the artist to quickly construct the parameters of the drawing.

Two-point perspective tends to concentrate the eye upon objects rather than on the space between them. Both vanishing points must be on the eye level and are usually so widely spaced that they are off the sheet. There are no parallel horizontal lines with two-point perspective (unlike single-point)

and hence the artist has to concentrate a little harder on the drawing. A drawing with a landscape layout (i.e. horizontal) normally lends itself to two-point perspective, and a portrait layout (i.e. vertical) to single-point.

With complex towns or groups of buildings, several vanishing points have to be constructed, at least in one's mind's eye, because the differently angled buildings will all require their own vanishing point. Since constructing the vanishing points is time consuming, it is better to visualize where

4.8 *The sense of perspective in this sketch has been enhanced by exaggerating the texture of the foreground steps. The telegraph lines also help with handling the sense of distance and change of direction at the top of the steps. The drawing is of Andraixt in Majorca.*

they are and check the angles in the field by using your pen or pencil as a guide. By holding the pen at the angle of the wall or roof and bringing it down to the paper via an arc rotated about your elbow, you should be able to check the logic of lines in perspective against how they appear in reality.

Although perspective deals primarily in angled lines, it is useful to remember that the weight of line, darkness of shadow and strength of colour also convey the appearance of distance. As a rule, objects in the foreground should have the thickest lines, the darkest shadow and the brightest colour, while those in the distance should have the reverse – that is, faint lines, soft shadows and subdued colour. Attention to such detail not only gives the townscape sketch a certain subtlety, but helps reinforce the sense of perspective established by the angled lines.

There are some further useful tips to add to the lessons of perspective drawing. One concerns windows: those disappearing some distance down the street need not be drawn as compressed rectangles; a simple vertical line will suffice. Likewise, if the detail of, say, paving is shown in the foreground, it is quite unnecessary to attempt to show it in the background, and a mere hint will be enough in the middle ground.

If you are going to depart from full scientific perspective drawing with its complicated rotating picture planes (not only cumbersome to put into practice, but unrealistic in the field), then you will have to use your eye to fix the depth of elements within the picture. The well-trained eye will in time prove as reliable as is necessary but you can assist it by using a pencil to establish the angle or proportion of height to width (in perspective). By holding the pencil and using the thumb as a sliding measure you should achieve accuracy to within 10%, which is good enough for location sketching. However, once you have established the bay width or the depth of the building and are happy with it visually (your measurements should always be checked against how it looks), then you will discover that the angle of the diagonal will remain constant. This will allow you to tackle complex subjects such as street arcades or the column spacings in the aisle of a church.

Diagonals can also be used to establish the centre of a wall or building in perspective. By striking both diagonals lightly in pencil (or just fixing them in one's mind), the centre is quickly obtained and hence other information such as the spacing of windows or location of a door can be added, knowing that the basic layout is correct.

The choice of eye level is important in perspective drawing. If you are interested, say, in the skyline of a tall building, then it pays to take as low an eye level as possible and render the silhouette of the top dark against a light sky. This is how the perspective artists of the 1930s presented their brash new skyscraper designs. Alternatively, if you are wishing to look 'into' the subject, then try to use a high eye level so that you can delve down into the streets and spaces and show how they relate to each other from this angle. When portraying a very tall building or lofty interior from the viewpoint of you gazing upwards, remember that there is a vertical vanishing point pulling the lines together high over your head. Such a drawing is really in single-point perspective, with you turned through 90°.

An understanding of perspective is a great aid to those intent upon drawing architecture and towns. Try not, however, to allow the rules to dictate your every move, for spontaneity and flair can be driven away by too slavishly following the academic conventions of perspective. Some recent graphic artists such as Paul Hogarth have deliberately broken such rules in order to arrest the eye and encourage it to dwell upon the subject longer. They have developed a system of superimposing objects in space which accords, to some extent, with Oriental concepts of perspective. However, beware that if you break the rules of perspective, a naivety creeps in which may undermine the overall appearance of the finished sketch, no matter how finely the details are rendered.

Chapter 5

Line and shade

Sketching the outline of objects can lead to rather featureless and abstract drawing. Although one may recognize the shape of a house, its value to us as an object is determined by issues of form, texture and arrangement. These qualities are best represented not by line alone, but through line and shade.

Shade gives a sense of three-dimensional reality to two-dimensional shapes. The convention is simple: select a direction for a source of light (often

5.1 *A simple line drawing is a good starting point for architectural exploration. Here a sketch plan is used to supplement the drawn view of Aylsham Church in Norfolk.*

imagined) and shade the sides of the object pointing away from the light source, drawing the shadow cast on to the ground and other surfaces. Your simple outline will then become alive with form, structure and surface richness. The more the building or object is modelled in plan or section, the greater will be the complexity of shade and shadows.

This convention becomes a reality when you draw on sunny days (mornings or afternoons are the best times to take advantage of angled light), but you can invent a source of strong light if it is not present. Ideally choose sunlight coming over your shoulder (preferably your left one) at an angle of 45°. This will make the most dull power station or comprehensive school suddenly dance off the page.

Many 18th- or 19th-century buildings employ cornices, string courses and window margins in order to create panels of walls and frames to highlight key architectural elements. The presence of these features can be emphasized in the sketch by exaggerating the play of light and shade on the façade. Similarly, modern buildings with their exposed structure and service runs also benefit from the use of this graphic technique. When drawing urban space or landscape design, shade and shadows create a necessary sense of substance

5.2 *These four sketches of a Victorian terrace of seaside flats in Dovercourt, Essex, show how a line drawing (a) can be enhanced by stippled shading (b), hatched shading (c), and pencil tone shading (d). In each case the formal composition is enhanced by shading.*

(a)

(b)

(c)

(d)

to things such as dwarf walls, hedges, trees and sculpture.

By placing elements in front of each other, shadows can be cast from one object on to another. The layering of objects in the picture not only enlivens the composition, but adds spatial complexity to the subject. Elements placed in front of a building such as lamp-posts, telephone boxes or trees give a sense of depth to the sketch and allow shadows to pass along the horizontal surfaces and up the vertical ones. By such means the distances in plan between

object and observer can be expressed and exploited graphically.

The function of shadows is, therefore, to make you aware of the depth within the view: they give flat two-dimensional subjects a semblance of reality. The rendition of shadows follows similar conventions to those of perspective. As a rule, darker shade and stronger shadows should be in the foreground of the sketch, becoming progressively lighter as they move into the distance. This has the effect of reinforcing the illusion of perspective.

5.3 *This pen drawing of the pioneer village of New Lanark, Scotland, uses shade to express the pedimented gable and to focus the eye upon the cupola.*

5.4 *Shade, shadow and perspective have been used to exploit the dramatic composition of this church square in Gaeta in Italy. Notice how the columns impose an enormous scale on the space, and how cafés enliven the perimeter of the town square.*

VISTA

5.5 *Simple pencil shading brings alive the three-dimensional qualities of the urban spaces in central Prague (near the top of Wenceslas Square in this instance). Here a distinction is made graphically between object buildings and the background architecture of the city.*

5.6 *The use of shade and shadow enhances the sculptural qualities of this coal mine at the Snowdown Colliery in Kent.*

5.7 *Line and shade are used to distinguish between dressed stone, rough stone, render and slate of the Royal Mile in Edinburgh.*

5.8 *These two sketches of Norfolk towns (Holt and Aylsham) employ a simple mixture of line, shade, pattern and texture. By mixing the four techniques, something of the quality of historic areas is captured.*

Chapter 6

Composition

An appreciation of composition is particularly important when drawing buildings and cities. The abstract nature of architecture means that sketches have to be well composed, otherwise the finished drawing may lack appeal, or fail to communicate the qualities that attracted you to the subject in the first place.

Generally speaking, the subject of the drawing should occupy the middle third of the sheet, not centrally placed, but perhaps positioned on the basis of the golden section. The proportional harmony of the golden section can enhance the drawing and give the subject a feeling of repose on the sheet. The subject can, of course, be in the foreground, middle ground or distance. It often helps, however, if the main object of the sketch is in the middle ground with foreground detail such as paving and background silhouette used to establish layers in the drawing.

Since buildings are made of materials of known size (bricks, blocks of stone, curtain walling, etc.), the opportunity often exists to exploit the rhythmic patterns they create. By considering the position of elements in the drawing it is often possible to create interesting arrangements which take advantage of the relative scale of the different building materials. Moreover, as we are all familiar with the dimensions of a standard brick, the use of

patterns of brick courses quickly establishes a sense of scale within the sketch.

Often it is possible to fill an area of the drawing with brickwork or tiling, and this can provide a texture to set against more detailed line work of, say, a Georgian window or doorcase. The justaposition of line, shadow and texture can make an attractive drawing, and it is worth taking time before starting the sketch to find a good combination of these elements. A little licence may also be permitted in rearranging the parts or extending (or exaggerating) the area of brickwork in order to produce a more satisfactory final drawing. Remember that good composition may also have been the architect or town planner's objective, and that your sketch is simply bringing out elements of the town scene which already exist, though perhaps looking slightly different in reality.

A good sketch should have layers of information and meaning. By setting elements into the foreground, especially those which give local character, you can convey the atmosphere of a street or urban area. Such details as post boxes, seats or cars expressing local character (a 2 cv in France, for instance, or a Fiat 500 in Italy) can be placed in the foreground, and this not only improves the composition of the sketch, but can give it extra complexity and richness. Remember, too, that

6.1 *This street scene in London benefits from details such as market stalls and a stripey canopy. This fine drawing (dated 1992) by Francis Tibbalds has layers of interest which help inform the subject.*

knowing what to leave out is also important. Unlike the literal documentation of the photographer, a drawing permits the artist to exercise a discerning eye, adding or subtracting detail to the benefit of the sketch.

Building designers play with various ingredients to produce a satisfactory piece of architecture. They have proportion, colour, outline, texture, harmony, shadow and framing at their disposal. Likewise, artists should seek out these qualities within the object or subject they are tackling, and exploit them in the drawing. After all, there is no better way of getting to know a subject than draw-

ing it, and no better way of remembering what it is really like beneath the surface appearance.

Some modern buildings are highly abstract in appearance and often rather minimal in detail. These buildings derive from the legacy of the International Style which began in the 1920s, and which put machine production and functional logic before craftmanship or individual human needs. Such buildings require a different approach to being rendered through architectural drawing than do more traditional townscapes. Here you will find a ruler useful and perhaps a circle template, and the use of dark shade and dramatic highlight-

6.2 *This sketch of a street in Florence focuses upon the walling elements and surface textures. The use of shade and shadow helps enhance the appearance of three dimensions, thereby better express-ing the main architec-tural components. Unnecessary detail has been left out.*

ing may also be in order. Similarly, small areas of bright colour may enliven the drawing, and give a dull building a focus of interest. Whatever drawing technique is employed, it is important to think hard about composition before starting to draw, and to try to enter into the spirit of the period of the subject before putting pencil to paper. An abstract modernist building may well suit a cool, almost cerebral, style of drawing. On the other hand, a Brutalist building of the 1960s, with a rough-textured concrete façade (as on the South Bank in London), would lend itself to a charcoal or a pencil drawing using a 6B to bring out the graininess of the surface. Architecture of whatever period has always attracted the artist, and modern buildings are no exception.

It is useful to try to relate the compositional arrangement of the sketch to the theme of the sub-ject. Should you be drawing a city church faced by a square, then both church and square should fig-ure in the sketch since both are probably there in support of each other. In Europe most cathedrals and many town churches are fronted at their west end by a square, and it would be foolish to draw the church without at least hinting at the presence of the square. Consequently, your composition should provide space for both, perhaps with church and

square linked by single-point perspective. As the square will probably be paved over and perhaps edged with clipped hedges or statues, the artist has elements around which to build up an attractive and well-constructed picture.

The relative positioning of the different ele-ments, the weight of line and tonal value of each are all important considerations and should be planned in advance of starting to draw. There is nothing worse than spending a great deal of time carefully drawing an ornate Baroque church to find that you have not captured the spirit of the place through not considering the composition of the picture with due care. Remember that a degree of abstraction or restraint is important – you cannot draw everything, and to select the focus of atten-tion at the outset is vital. This should prevent you from overworking the subject and ending up pro-ducing what amounts to a second-rate photograph.

Since the most prominent features of a building are those which form a frame (doors, windows, trusses, gateways), you should incorporate these into your picture. As we move through a building, we have an impression of prospects opening out of bigger rooms viewed through narrow spaces. The transition between rooms is often marked by a doorway which is deliberately framed. Since we

6.3 *By placing the 'subject' of the sketch (which here depicts the Merchant City, Glasgow) near the top of the drawing, the spaces which form the context and public realm are also described.*

6.4 *This drawing of the semicircular portico to Bramante's S. Maria dell Pace in Rome leaves much detail out in order to express the framing of the doorway and the clash between curved and straight lines.*

experience architecture by passing through these framing elements, they are very much part of the scene and therefore cannot be ignored. Indeed, successful sketches frequently tantalize the observer with a glimpse of a distant, and sometimes mysterious, world through such 'frames' – the view through the solid gateway of a medieval town being a good example.

As with all great buildings or fine cities and landscapes, there needs to be an element of complexity and richness in the freehand drawing. Such complexity can be set against the plainness of unadorned surfaces to heighten the drama of the sketch. Alternatively, any repeated surface decoration can establish a rhythm or beat as in music. Searching out such compositions can result in well-informed drawing which not only sustains our attention but teaches us something about the nature of the place.

As mentioned already, the positioning on the page of the main subject of the sketch is important. A sketch can be either landscape (horizontal)

6.5 *The cliff-like structure of the ferry* Norland *is broken up by the angled lines of mooring ropes and access gangway. Placing the bollard in the foreground adds to the layers of interest which reinforce the nautical theme of the sketch.*

Beacon Hill Boston, Mass. BEdwards 1971

6.6 The Beacon Hill area of Boston, Massachusetts, contains fine 19th-century houses and squares. Here railings and a fire hydrant add foreground interest and give the sketch a complexity which a study of building façades alone would lack.

6.7 This sketch of an advertising gable in Ukiah, California, uses the telegraph pole, wires and parked cars to add further layers of meaning or character. The nature of American urban design was the starting point for this descriptive drawing.

6.8 *Mackintosh carefully composes his drawings. In this sketch (dated 1905) of a barn in Suffolk he superimposes elevations, details and perspective views both to inform the viewer and enliven the page. (Glasgow University: Mackintosh Collection)*

or portrait (vertical) in layout, depending upon whether a panorama or, for instance, a street scene is preferred. Panoramas of cities can be dull affairs – just a collection of roofs and towers – though vertical elements such as columnar cypress trees, factory chimneys or masts can be used to offset the stretching horizontality of the subject. Likewise, street scenes may require some horizontality or shallow-angled lines to counter the tendency

towards the vertical. In both cases you should search out shapes and lines to balance the dominant 'direction' of subject or layout.

To return to the subject of the town church; if you wish to draw the square in any detail, then it is necessary to place the church towards the top of the sheet. This will allow you to pull the lines of the square and its paving towards you, thereby giving the impression that you are looking both 'into' the space and 'at' the church. This type of drawing establishes a dialogue between object and space, and allows you to consider how the square is used and decorated.

Often a good sketch consists of leaving large areas of the sheet relatively unrendered. A mere hint of lines is usually sufficient and the openness of approach on one part of the page can enhance the level of detail elsewhere. A common mistake is to draw to the same level of intensity right across the sheet, thereby removing the opportunity for tensional conflicts. Since traditional architecture plays on such tensions (for example, the contrast between a decorated entrance doorway and a plain area of wall) and modern architecture often ignores them, a perceptive drawing should seek to exploit these differences.

Try, if you can, to compose your drawing around powerful lines of force within the sketch. These may be the vertical ribs of an office block, the diagonal grid of a steel-framed bridge, or the flowing lines of forestry planting. The structure of a drawing should consist of these dominating linear forces being mediated by secondary lines or areas of shadow. If possible, seek a balance between the primary and secondary elements, or at least soften the harsh linearity of most architectural subjects by drawing in surface pattern or texture.

The inclusion of such elements as people, cars or vegetation helps to counteract the rectangular or linear forms of buildings. The degree to which these secondary elements soften the sharp outlines of architecture depends upon the subject and the effect sought. You may wish to add complexity and contradiction to the subject, or simply accept the realities of a highly engineered environment.

The play between horizontal and vertical lines, and between hard and soft elements, can be developed into triangular groupings on the sheet. By having three points of interest the picture is more easily composed. Instead of, say, the unresolved dominance of the towering lines of a skyscraper, the drawing will have a repose which may suit certain subjects. Triangular framing does require rather more than a simple sketch; the artist is now moving towards a more detailed drawing, perhaps as a prelude to easel painting.

As so much urban drawing deals with the façades of buildings, the artist should try to add interest to the drawing by giving the observer a sense of looking both into the spaces of the city and at its buildings. The effect can be achieved by pulling the lines of a street or square towards the observer, thereby creating space which is 'entered into'. The tension which results from the city as 'elevation' and the street as 'stage' can lead to a sketch rich in ideas about the nature of urban design.

6.9 *Landscape drawing provides an opportunity to frame views. Here a distant church spire in a village near Warwick nestles in a hollow with mature oaks and pines directing the line of vision towards it.*

Chapter 7

The importance of practice

The co-ordination of hand and eye is a necessary starting point for freehand drawing. It is only through frequent practice and by following sound principles that the facility to draw without hesitation or uncertainty can be attained. The fluid, confident lines of an accomplished draughtsman are achieved as the result of much practice. This book does not pretend to teach drawing, only to encourage its use as part of the design process. Like the acquisition of all skills, training and self-discipline are as important as the possession of natural talent.

Practice does not require that you spend your time entirely on location drawing. The home and the design studio or workshop provide ample

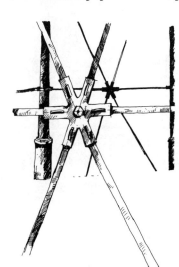

7.1 *Small subjects can be a useful starting point in learning to explore through freehand drawing. Here a fragment of structure from the lighthouse at Dovercourt forms the basis of the sketch.*

opportunity to develop eye-to-hand co-ordination or to test the rules of perspective drawing. By looking at the outline of the subject and infilling part or all of the detail – whether it be a drawing of a chair or cup and saucer – you will quickly develop the basic skills necessary for sketching in the street. The importance of spontaneous, relaxed drawing cannot be overemphasized. While you might be concentrating on organizing the angled lines of a scene into a sound perspective framework, the fact that you are sketching at all is of the greatest importance. Unlike the first notes on a piano or trumpet, the artist's scribbles are largely a private affair and should not disturb the household. It is remarkable how quickly most people graduate from producing primitive, inhibited sketches to life-like representations.

It is important that you approach drawing from both ends – from the personal, idiosyncratic angle, and from the point of view of academic skill. The latter concerns questions of perspective, composition, shade and shadow. By developing both a personal style and a good grasp of basic principles, it should be possible to produce drawings which are lively and informative. Architectural sketching benefits from both a strong individual approach to the subject and the necessary graphic techniques to relay the private vision satisfactorily.

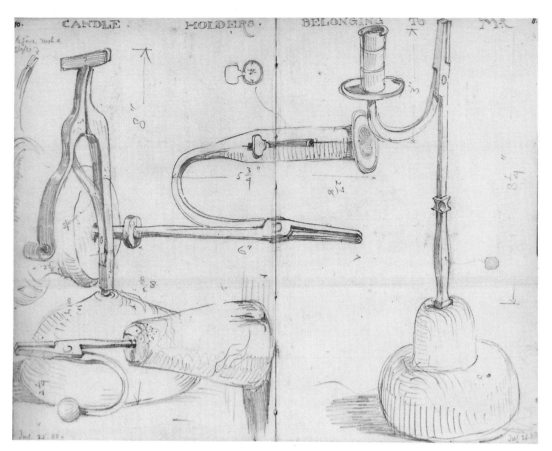

7.2 Edward May's sketch of candleholders is the type of subject which lends itself to a practice exercise. May's facility for drawing was, no doubt, acquired as the result of many such sketches. (RIBA Drawings Collection)

7.3 This simple sketch of an irregular urban space near Wenceslas Square in Prague was prepared in order to demonstrate the effect of the gateway block and the termination of the vista by a circular gable. Sketches like this need only take a few minutes and must necessarily leave out a great deal of detail. It is also the basis for figure 5.5.

7.4 *This sketch (dated 1905) by Mackintosh of a hall at Cley in Norfolk edits out features in an attempt to interpret rather than merely describe the scene. The artist's facility is achieved as the result of practice and a critical approach. (Glasgow University: Mackintosh Collection)*

7.5 *A degree of abstraction helps when rendering difficult subjects, as in this sketch made near Dubrovnik.*

DECONSTRUCTED LANDSCAPE : BIRMINGHAM 1992   BWE

7.6 *Derelict industrial areas (in this case on the edge of Birmingham) provide much material upon which to practise different drawing techniques.*

Chapter 8

From the sketch to plan making and documentary investigation

Sketching may on occasion be supplemented by drawing quick plans or sections. The sketch is a useful and enjoyable tool, but there are occasions when more analytical drawings are required. Although a sketch can indicate the position of a doorway relative to the rest of the façade, it cannot show the importance of the door with regard to the plan of the building. Here you will have to resort to preparing drawings of a more technical nature.

As with sketching, there are a few useful tips to bear in mind. If you are going to measure the subject, get someone else to hold the end of the tape measure, and preferably a third person to read out the dimensions. Your task will then be that of drawing and recording the measurements. Any plan prepared in this way should have the sketch plan, section or elevation drawn at the same time as the measurements are taken, and ideally at the same scale.

Height often poses a problem, but you can triangulate the subject or alternatively use a staircase (if you have access to the interior) to take a vertical measure. Sometimes you can count the number of brick courses, assuming they are laid at four courses per foot. If these fail, then it is possible to take an informed guess on the basis of 9 feet (2.7 metres) per storey for an ordinary house (allowing for the type of construction) and 15 feet (4.4 metres) for a grander building.

The sketch plan does not have to be dimensionally accurate to contain useful information. The fact that the building is square in plan, or that a city street is the same width as the height of houses enclosing it, is more important than mere dimensions. You may be able to pace out the dimensions of the building, on the assumption that your step is about 3 feet (0.9 metres), or determine the height of doors by your reach.

The use of approximate plans is to supplement the sketched information and to help bring some aspect of the design into clearer focus. After all, you are sketching to learn about the built environment, and learning does require a disciplined approach. With townscape sketches, a quickly drawn plan of the figure-ground (the relationship between the solids of buildings and the voids of streets and spaces) helps explain the geometry or pattern evident in your view. It may also encourage you to draw from another point in the street, thereby helping you to reach a real understanding of the often complex spatial interactions in an urban scene.

Assuming you have prepared a sketch and supplemented this with a plan or section, then you may decide to take your investigation further.

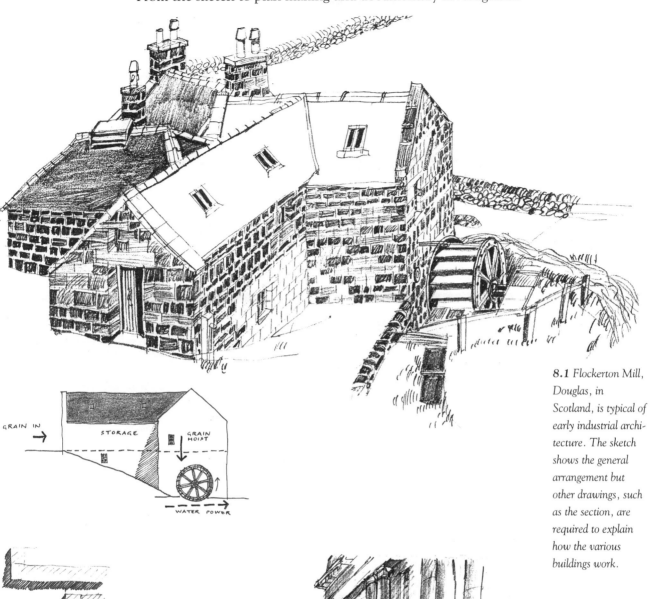

GRAIN IN

STORAGE

GRAIN HOIST

WATER POWER

8.1 *Flockerton Mill, Douglas, in Scotland, is typical of early industrial architecture. The sketch shows the general arrangement but other drawings, such as the section, are required to explain how the various buildings work.*

8.2 *The sketch of the Royal Crescent in Bath is supplemented by a plan drawn at the time from memory. The exploration of the geometry of the volumes at an urban level was the reason for the drawing.*

8.3 *This sketch, based upon field notes and town plans, shows the proportional system employed at the Baroque Piazza San Carlo in Turin. Plan, section and elevation have all been employed to highlight the relationship between the detail and the whole.*

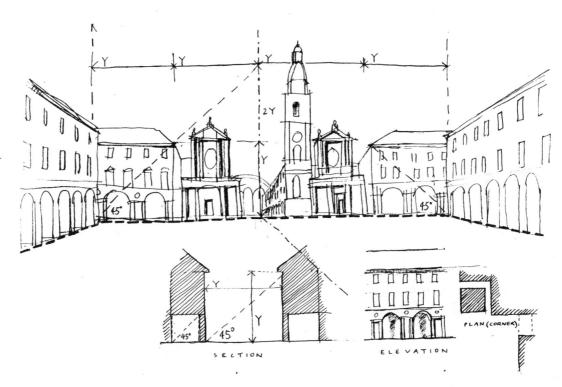

8.4 *Figure-ground drawings prepared from a good map can show the relationship between the solids (buildings) and voids (spaces) of the city. Here an area of London Docklands is shown with the lack of connections between old and new communities manifested through the drawing technique.*

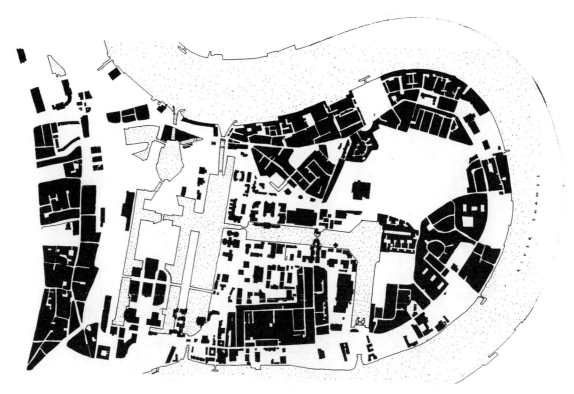

8.5 The urban structure of the market place in Holt, Norfolk, is explored through this figure-ground study. The original outline of the square is clearly shown. Buildings within the central space are later encroachments.

Local libraries will probably contain documentary records about the date of the subject or other information which can enhance your understanding of the area you have studied through the sketch. Inquiry through graphic analysis is a useful means of cultivating an appreciation of an area or subject, particularly if it then leads to a search through archival records or historic plans. This may not suit everybody's needs, but for a school or college project the bringing together of graphic and written sources is a useful educational tool.

Just as in your freehand drawing, the weight of line must be used to help explain aspects of the plan. The sketch plans are meant to communicate and thus should abide by accepted norms of technical drawing. Hence the most important information (such as the position of the walls of a house) should be rendered in the thickest lines and deepest tones. If the garden fence and structural walls have the same weight of line, then their relative importance is obscured. Likewise, the presence of mouldings on the front façade may be important to

understanding the proportional rules which the original architect employed (as with a Georgian house), and this fact can be drawn to the attention of the viewer by your selection of an appropriate weight of line. The presence or absence of lines and their relative weight is as important as the presence or absence of words in a report.

Your sketches and plans are really records of facts or your interpretation of them – they are not mere speculations or whimsical invention. If you wish to move into design changes, then your inventions should be clearly indicated. The progression from sketch as record, plan as description, and design drawing as proposed change is an accepted method of proceeding. But it is important that should you mix all three together on a single sheet; then this fact should be communicated to those who look at the drawing. Similarly, records of fact and matters of interpretation should be clearly marked as such and not combined in the same graphic language.

The intention is to supplement the sketch with

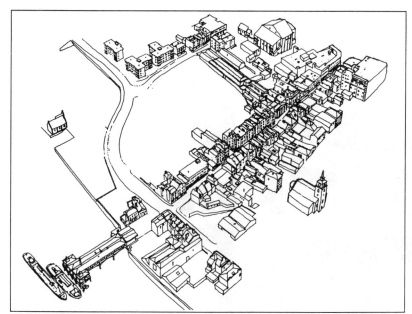

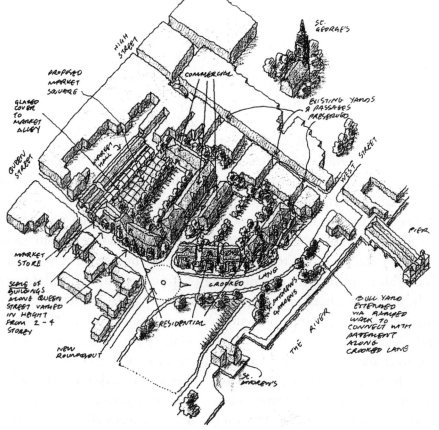

8.6 *These studies (dated 1991) of Gravesend in Kent by Richard Reid move from sketchbook drawings to more analytical explorations and broad design proposals.*

other relevant information. Your need for additional material will in all probability stem from a practical consideration such as curiosity about how the building is constructed, how the landscape is formed, or the design put together. Hence, the initial sketch – itself probably the result of a need to admire or record – leads to further inquiry which takes you from the sketchbook to the notepad and perhaps to the local archive office, planning department or library. Seen in this way, the sketch is part of the process of understanding, not an end in itself.

Through the sketchbook we may learn to appreciate objects and places for what they are, and as

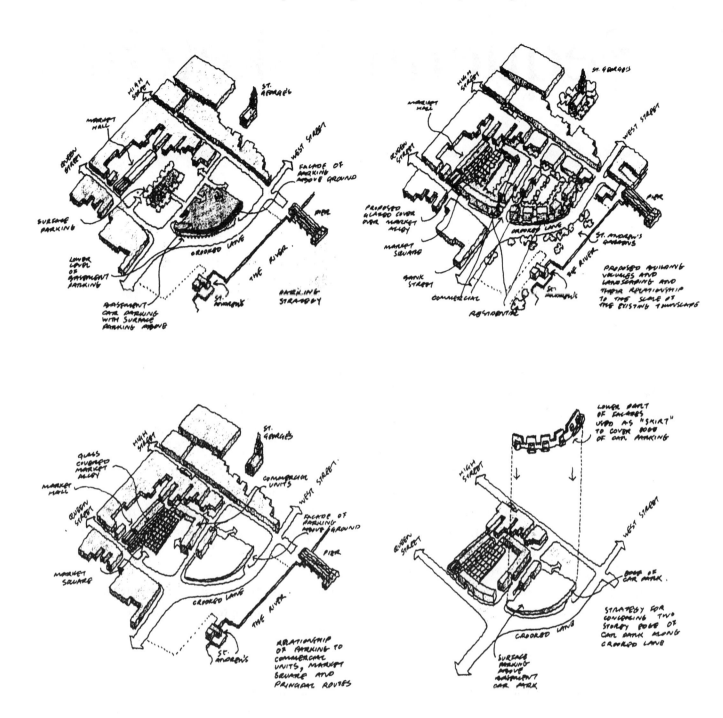

designers intervene in a more informed and sensitive fashion. Because the sketchbook requires our concentrated involvement and can lead outwards into the further investigations mentioned above, it is a great deal more useful than the camera. The camera can only record – it cannot edit, select or interpret. A trained photographer may use the camera creatively, but its educational benefits are limited. By encouraging us to become more visually literate through the countless photographs produced each year, the camera has had the adverse effect of focusing our attention upon the superficialities of subject and form, rather than upon their underlying structure and meaning.

Chapter 9

Sequential sketches

Sketching is about exploration, about learning to see places and architecture through the graphic experience. As such, the architectural illustrator is concerned with interpretation rather than mere description, and that interpretation must contain elements of critical judgement. A common mistake is to draw too literally and to seek representation from one viewpoint alone.

To reach a real understanding of 'place', you need to walk through it, thereby experiencing the changing geometries of the urban scene. Sketching can be a useful aid to urban analysis as long as the viewpoints are chosen with some thought. The most rewarding urban spaces often revolve around a public monument where a mixture of squares, streets and lanes provide a range of spatial patterns. As you move through the different volumes, you become aware of large and small spaces, enclosed and partially enclosed ones, connected and unconnected ones. The beauty of many towns, particularly historic ones, lies in this variety and in the unexpected delights which unfold.

You can attempt to record such experiences through a single sketch, but usually a collection of sketches is more informative. The mystery of old towns, which derives in no small part from the irregular street layout, and the marvellous contrast between large public buildings and small domestic ones, can be captured in a well-planned sequence of analytical sketches. The complexity of such places and the subtle interplay between the parts means that three or four sketches are required to capture the essence of the place and its changing geometries. Such sequential sketches (or 'serial vision', as Gordon Cullen put it) should be based upon well-selected viewpoints. For the drawing of a historic town with a major public monument as focus you should sketch:

- the approach from afar, or at least just outside the immediate sphere of influence of the monument;
- a view glimpsed of the monument above roof tops or along streets (the monument should not yet be fully in view);
- a view showing much or all of the monument within its setting;
- a close-up view of the monument, with steps, railings and human activity round about.

Whatever sequence you follow (and many different vistas are normally available), it is important to keep the feeling of mystery and suspense alive. Therefore the story should unfold like a good play with each drawing an act which develops a particular theme. It often helps if the views selected are

Sequential sketches

9.1 This sequence of four views along a route in Siena seeks to explore the landmarking of a street by major and minor architectural 'events'.

9.2 *These four drawings take the theme of exploring bridge crossings over the canals of Venice. Each sketch relates the bridges to the adjoining palace façades.*

of, or appear alongside, 'hinge' buildings which act as key 'events' in the unfolding of the urban experience. Gateways provide an obvious example, but often steps or a café are equally useful to aid the observer. Few major towns are without such a sequence of spaces and key buildings, and to search them out through the sketchbook is a valuable and enjoyable experience. Sadly many modern places are without these qualities and the designer's task today is how to introduce greater spatial variety into an otherwise dull network of streets.

If you are seeking to analyse urban space through such means, you may find sketch plans useful. They can help relate your sketches to key factors in the

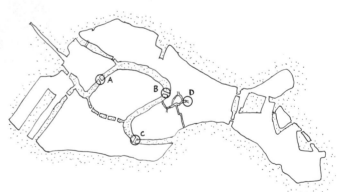

9.3 *This sequence of sketches presents the village of Easdale in Scotland. The views selected describe critical points – from the sea edge to inner spaces. The emphasis is upon entry, harbourside, procession and termination – all studied against a Highland backcloth.*

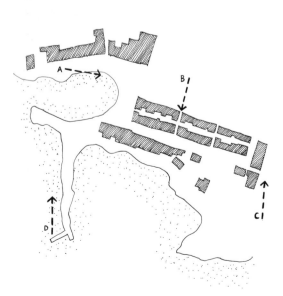

9.4 *The curving line of the building fronts facing the beach in Cromer, Norfolk, takes advantage of the clifftop. Notice how the line is punctuated by the occasional gable, oriel window and verandah.*

structure of the town, and explain dynamic or spatial relationships which were only hinted at in the street view.

By using sequential sketches to analyse urban scenes, you will quickly become aware of the complex geometries present. Slight deviations in routes or changes in level can be quite marked in reality, though they seem hardly discernable in plan or section. Likewise, abrupt changes of direction can break the line of continuity that is so important in the enjoyment of place. Contrast can be employed deliberately and should be reserved for siting significant public buildings such as the sudden termination of a vista by a town hall or the set-back on a street to reveal a church. Often, however, the use of contrast is abused by private buildings such as a supermarket or an office block seeking to draw attention to itself.

You can, of course, record contrast through a discerning sketch. If your sketches are concerned with contrast and discontinuity, then do not hesitate to underline the point with a well-selected viewpoint. For example, if you find that the scale of the town

changes at a particular point, then this is where to draw. By placing the large and small buildings side by side their full impact may be felt, and if the change of scale occurs at a change of direction (which is often the case), then the sketch has additional value. Sequential sketches should therefore seek out differences and contrasts in order to enliven the drawings and increase your own awareness of design issues.

Sequential sketches can also be employed to explore the line of continuity referred to above and found in many urban situations. Such lines often unite a row of warehouses facing a harbourside or the frontage of buildings along a high street. It is often important to maintain such continuity (for reasons of civic design) in order to provide a firm edge to the urban scene. A straight line tends to be less satisfactory visually than one which curves slightly or absorbs some irregularity with ease. A sketch of such a line, whether straight or curving, can be quite delightful and informative, especially if it is part of a sequence of related views which deal also with questions of punctuation – in other words, how the line is stopped and defined along its route.

It is important for the observer to 'read' the line and its punctuation, otherwise the point of the sketch may be lost. Therefore try to highlight the elements which make up the line of continuity, and draw attention to the elements which define points along its length. You are trying to make 'informed' sketches – sketches which tell you about the nature of urban design – so a measure of selectivity and focus in your drawing is important.

If the line of continuity links together the façades of a group of buildings facing a river, then use a particular tone or wash to unite them in your sketch. Add contrast or complexity by drawing attention to certain ingredients within the view such as decorated doorways, special shopfronts or town churches. Your sequence of sketches should explore progress along the line, noting where and how it is broken, deflected or punctuated.

Mention has already been made of the geometry of urban spaces. Most places of interest contain a mixture of cubes, rectangles and spheres. Such complex geometrics are the essence of attractive townscape. These spaces and their interrelationships can only be discovered by walking about the town and recording one's impressions in the sketchbook. The volumetric geometry often extends to the interiors of buildings where a circular space inside, say, a church is complemented by a rectangle of urban space outside. In his design for the Sheldonian Theatre in Oxford, Sir Christopher Wren played upon such interrelationships, as did the designers of many Baroque churches in Rome.

You can train your eye to recognize and appreciate this architectural interplay, and through the sketchbook record and analyse your experiences. Of course, if you are an architect, town planner or developer, you may be in a position to bring this sensibility to bear upon current civic design. Europe once had a splendid tradition of related interior and exterior spaces, but the car and the dominance of street traffic have together eroded our perception of this rich urban heritage.

Part Three
Case Studies in
Drawing

Chapter 10

Towns, townscapes and squares

An appreciation of landscape – the aesthetic quality of the countryside – has been part of our culture for at least two hundred years, but its urban equivalent – townscape – is a relative newcomer. The urban theorist and graphic delineator of towns Gordon Cullen drew our attention to 'townscape' in a series of articles in the *Architectural Review* about 30 years ago. His subsequent book, *The Concise Townscape*, remains a valuable introduction to the subject. What Cullen and others have sought to show is that towns have aesthetic qualities just as rich as the countryside, and that the recording and preservation of the poetry of the urban scene is as important as protecting the beauties of the landscape.

What then makes up the beauty of towns, both ancient and modern? Different theories prevail, especially between urban theorists of a European as against American bent. On the whole, we are dealing with the following key qualities, each worthy of exploration through the sketchbook:

* squares, enclosed places and centres of activity;
* routes through the town such as streets, alleyways, lanes and footpaths;
* landmarks of varying types such as church spires, high office buildings and transmitter masts.

These important elements of urban character are supported by a secondary layer of features that provide rhythm, patterning and changes of scale or punctuation. Hence we may find that a pattern running through the glazing of an office building is echoed in the paving of a square at its base: façade and space are thus united by a commonality of line.

The sketchbook is a useful tool for understanding towns and cultivating an awareness of the complex visual language of the city. Unlike the countryside, many cities, especially big modern ones, are very complicated; their spatial structure may be disjointed and the skyline a battleground for different styles. In spite of this, the freehand sketch is a useful starting point for analysis. As when drawing a landscape, one has to be selective, and it is best to avoid a too literal representation of the urban scene. A good townscape drawing focuses upon relationships and highlights the crucial elements such as the street line, silhouette and entry point.

Whether one is drawing countryside or a town, establishing the structure of the view is of great importance. The relationship of hedges and trees to a field in the landscape sketch is analogous to that of buildings and towers to a street in the townscape drawing. To focus upon the windows and doors of the buildings is akin to a precise rendition of the leaves and branches of a hedge – such detail may not be necessary to your analysis.

Rather than seek to sketch the full complexity of a town, it is best to concentrate on the key elements listed earlier. In this way the artist (or student) will better understand the main factors that shape our perception of cities, and, as an urban designer, will be better informed as to how and when to change their form or structure. Let us begin by looking at the first of the key elements: squares, enclosed spaces and centres of activity.

Cities do not contain an even distribution of social or commercial activity. Most towns have squares where people meet, civic functions are held and where railway and bus stations often make their presence felt. As focal points, 'squares' come in many forms and sizes; some are regular, others charmingly irregular and uneven. As our perception of cities is shaped by our memory of squares (such as Trafalgar Square in London, Times Square in New York or George Square in Glasgow), they perform a vital function in making one place feel different from another.

Squares are essentially enclosed spaces, though they can be partly open at the edges and partly filled by buildings. The degree of enclosure is important, however, for a real civic focus requires a space which is 'contained' by the surrounding buildings. Containment places a responsibility on the enclosing structures to be of sufficient size to prevent the space spilling out. If the square is very large, then the surrounding buildings need to be fairly high, and any breaks in the continuity of the façades filled, unless the breaks lead to further events of interest such as a secondary square or a public building set back from the main square.

It is important when drawing squares and courtyards to allow some of the character of the place to invade the sketch. For example, if it is a residential square, then to incorporate such details as washing lines or children playing would not only enliven the sketch, but inform its content as well. Alternatively, if the subject is a public square, then

10.1 *The relationship between public building, public square and gathering space is the basis of this drawing of Rome in Italy.*

10.2 *The deliberate landmarking of the street junction is a common feature of 19th-century urban design. Here in a tenement neighbourhood of Glasgow the architect for the church placed a Gothic spire as near to the pavement edge as he could. The coherence of the scene is the result of four-storey height limits placed on the builders of the tenements by the Victorian city council.*

elements of a civic nature such as statues or trees planted in formal lines should be included. You may wish to add people since this gives life to the square, but be careful to draw people appropriate to the location and select such details as local costume to bring a touch of *genius loci*.

Whatever type of square or courtyard you decide to draw, ensure that the sketch has a focus. Drawings of squares tend to be sketches of spaces (not objects) and hence can have a vacuous quality. The reality may be that the square itself lacks a focal point, but often you can overcome the problem by drawing a length of building façade to provide a point of interest around which to compose the sketch of the square. The building façade will probably be the principal frontage facing the square – perhaps a town church, market building or railway station. A great deal of effort will have to be devoted to sketching this properly as it is likely to be the major event within the space.

Once the focal point has been fixed, the rest of the sketch should fall into place with railings, fountains, statues, steps and walls providing useful articulation of the space. Often squares have more interesting paving details than do the surrounding roads, and these should be included in the sketch. Such details bring the foreground towards the viewer, and help establish the shape and configuration of the square. Equally, squares are frequently planted with interesting trees and shrubs whose foliage can provide much fascinating detail to set against the hard-edged buildings. Your sketch should demonstrate how good urban design consists of considering the buildings, spaces and landscape of the city as one, rather than as separate entities.

Squares which are distorted or uneven in shape can be more taxing to draw than regular ones. Remember that although the walls are not parallel, they have vanishing points along the same eye

10.3 The relationship between densely packed private houses, the castle and topography is the subject of this study of an Italian hill town. Here 'townscape' is analogous to 'landscape'.

10.4 *The Plaça Reial in Barcelona is an even-shaped square surrounded by buildings of consistent style and filled with splendid palm trees. Openings into the square at regular intervals allow it to connect with the older pattern of streets outside. By selecting certain elements, this elaborate civic space becomes manageable to draw.*

10.5 *Shops and pubs are traditionally grouped around market squares, as in this sketch of North Walsham in Norfolk.*

10.6 *Cloisters are often peaceful and well-shaded places to draw. Here in Barcelona Cathedral the central space is filled with luxurious planting overlooked by grotesque gargoyles.*

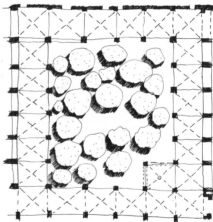

level. You may find, however, that one side of the square is strictly geometric in layout and often has buildings of fine proportion. You should exploit the differences in your sketch – contrasting the regular with the unplanned, thereby capturing the charm of the place.

Squares come in all sizes, from small domestic courtyards to broad civic spaces. The latter are the hardest to draw since they contain much complex detail and are often so wide that the sketches become panoramas. Beginners should start with small spaces and only attempt scenes such as London's Parliament Square after much practice.

If you do attempt a big public square, then a grasp of perspective is essential. However, scientific perspective may not provide all the answers in terms of composition or for capturing the action within the square. Here you may choose to adopt a more personal system of representing space, not unlike the Oriental system of perspective, which sets images (represented with no regard for geometric accuracy) layered in front of each other so that they become larger the nearer they are to the observer. With large squares, no matter which technique of perspective is employed, it is often instructive to try to enter into the space through the medium of drawing. If the artist chooses a position, not so much on the edge of the square looking in, but within the square and surrounded by its action, then something of the character will come through. Photomontage can also be employed to represent the background architecture, thereby allowing you to focus upon the activity in the square.

The most interesting urban spaces are those surrounded by buildings such as shops, cafés or bars. If the activities of these places are encouraged to spill out on to the square, so much the better. In addition, the square will frequently be edged by an arcade containing shops and restaurants. Hence the square is surrounded by buildings which respond in form to the activities that it encloses, providing a richness of visual and social detail at the perimeter of the space. It is unfortunate that these traditional qualities have been eroded by the ubiquitous presence of the car, which in many

10.7 *This domestic courtyard in Dubrovnik has the necessary accompaniments of family life prominently displayed in the shared space between the houses. The steps provide a hint of extra privacy – a point reinforced by the tubs of plants.*

European cities has usurped the city dweller from the city spaces.

Squares with much activity around the edge often have a focus of attention in the centre. Fountains, seats, an area for gossip under a few trees form the centre of many European civic spaces. In Britain it is more common to find a group of large plane trees growing within a railed-off enclosure. The relationship between the geometry of the space, its activities and planting are excellent subjects for a sketchbook analysis. Often there is room within the square for the internal activities of the enclosing buildings to spread well into the space. If a railway or underground station is located on the edge of the square, then its influence will be felt more directly than in the case of a café. Now there will be bustle and bursts of movement – at rush hours and when trains arrive. A similar situation can occur if a theatre faces a square; the times of the performance will be reflected in an increase of activity in the square.

One lesson to be drawn from this exploration is the need to allow perimeter functions to influence the design and layout of the square. A circulating system of roads prevents the peripheral traffic from spreading into the centre of the square, leaving the space free for, and enriched by, social interaction.

Those who design public buildings and railway stations have a responsibility to provide related urban space for this essential human need. It is a daunting task to try to draw a busy square, but to demonstrate the relationship between physical form and civilized values through the well-aimed sketch is useful, even if the drawing itself is a failure artistically.

Since squares are generally enclosed on all sides, the artist should employ shade and shadow to create the impression of spatil containment. You can use your imagination when portraying the direc-

10.8 Steps, alleyways and angled roads lead into this quiet square in San Felice Circeo in northern Italy. Columns and verandahs are used to give a measure of civic status to the space. The uneven drying of the watercolour was a deliberate attempt to capture the nature of the wall finishes.

10.9 *The courtyard formed at the rear of ancient tenements in the Old Town of Edinburgh offers a quiet space to experiment with sketching.*

10.10 *The fountain at this monastery in Dubrovnik provides the path with a sense of focus and deflects movement to either side.*

10.11 *Deep shadows are used to help explain the structure of this small square in Florence.*

tion of light in order express the quality of the square in the most favourable way. A deep shadow to left or right allows figures, statues or trees to be set against it, thereby standing out and creating a real feeling of occupying the space. Shading should not generally be drawn upon the focal building – the intention is to direct the eye towards it by masking out surrounding buildings. The focal building (say, a theatre or church) can have broken shadow or shade beneath lintels and cornices, but the principal structure in the square is best bathed in sunshine (even if this is not present in reality) and framed by other buildings and trees in shadow.

Sometimes a mixture of wash or conté crayon and fine line are the best materials to delineate such spaces. The wash or crayon depicts the shadows, while the line work can be employed for portraying decorative or principal elements. With complex urban spaces it pays to simplify the subject as far as possible, and to build up the sketch gradually, aiming to stop before the subject becomes overworked.

As squares are one of the chief attractions of towns, it is worth spending more time in them than elsewhere. The culture of cities often resides in the squares – a culture not just of architecture but of people and public functions. Lesser squares and domestic spaces are also valuable and provide important social centres for smaller districts. These secondary spaces may be a useful starting point for those intent upon understanding urban design, as drawing skills can be learnt in them unimpeded by the bustle or embarrassment that can arise in more central locations. For the lessons provided by urban spaces – those of entry, containment and perimeter activity – are to be gained equally well in small squares as in large ones.

These lesser squares show that a hierarchy of urban spaces exist in most towns. The civic square is a truly public space, while domestic squares set back from the street edge are more intimate in character, though often different again from semi-private squares land-locked within the middle of a city block. Hence the different types of enclosed urban spaces have distinctive qualities which relate to their levels of privacy and need for security. An informed sketch should communicate some of these differences in character.

Chapter 11

Streets, lanes and footpaths

Our movement through towns is normally along streets and roads, and hence our perception of the quality of place is shaped by what we see from them. Anybody intent upon exploring cities through the freehand sketch should, therefore, concentrate upon the routes people normally take. These vary from grand streets to alleyways and pedestrian footpaths, and each has its distinctive character. The different types of city street can be categorized as follows:

- *street* a relatively formal route lined by continuous frontages of buildings;
- *boulevard* a grander version of the street, often containing trees planted in parallel rows, and sometimes with a central reservation;
- *road* an informal car-dominated route generally of a suburban nature;
- *lane* an access route often serving the rear of properties and frequently running parallel to a street;

11.1 This formal street in Glasgow enclosed by late 19th-century tenements has a regimented character which extends through architecture, urban layout and planting design.

11.2 Access lanes (as here in Siena) are often tortuous routes which have grown up from ancient cart tracks. In this sketch the buildings over-shadow the lane which provides no space for gatherings of any description.

- *alleyway* a narrow route, often a service corridor originally constructed for the movement of carts;
- *footpath* a pedestrian-scale route between buildings, often an ancient right of way and known by a variety of local names such as a 'loke' in Norfolk or 'pend' in Edinburgh.

The mixture of different types of route within a town, and the way they connect up with each other and to the public squares, expresses the very essence of urban character. Not only is the spatial experience of using them enhanced by their variety and complexity (explore, for example, the Rows in Brighton), but you will often find that key routes are landmarked by important buildings. These points of punctuation help city dwellers to find their way around and to relate one set of routes to another.

Landmarks along routes come in many forms, from a distinctive 'event' such as a decorated pub jutting into the space, to an oriel window overlooking a change of direction, or a lofty church spire. One can search out these 'highlighting' features and describe them through the sketchbook. Many major routes through a town are deliberately punctuated by a well-placed statue or public building, but the lesser routes are often accidentally landmarked. Hence a hierarchy of landmarks may exist, each tailored to the scale of the route and its civic status.

If you are intent upon sketching a route, it is important to allow the drawing to focus upon or acknowledge a point of punctuation. Although the sketch may be concerned with the nature of a street or road, the fact that it has a landmark along it which provides local interest should not be overlooked. With long routes the points of punctuation allow us not only to measure how far we have travelled, but to experience the process of movement. On an urban motorway, tall or distinctive structures may provide distance markers, and the same is true on a pedestrian-scale alleyway.

Our route along a street can be intentionally punctuated by such features as a clock mounted on a bracket above our heads, or by a colonnaded entrance jutting into the pavement. Such manipulation of our perception by well-placed markers was normally reserved for public architecture, but today it is common to find illuminated advertisements or supermarket frontages exploiting these qualities.

Whether your sketch seeks to analyse a traditional route and its landmarks or a modern one, the same rules apply. Select a good vantage point, compose the drawing in your mind before you

11.3 *Here footpaths, lanes and roads meet with the church spire providing a landmark over the rooftops. This scene of Aylsham, Norfolk, is typical of English country towns.*

11.4 *The bracket-mounted clock at the Guildhall in Guildford provides an obvious point of punctuation along the main street. Notice also how the cupola is pushed to the edge of the roof to provide another landmark.*

11.5 *This attractive scene in Sperlonga in Italy shows how changes of level can be handled along a pedestrian route. Clues to where the pathway leads are marked by archways with doorways providing a secondary focus.*

11.6 *The archway above this street in Siena signifies where a territorial edge occurs and the steps further on are designed as private, not public, space.*

11.7 *The network of lanes, steps and footpaths in this stretch of an Italian hill town provide the basic urban structure around which more recent houses are grouped. Walls are an important element where abrupt changes of level occur.*

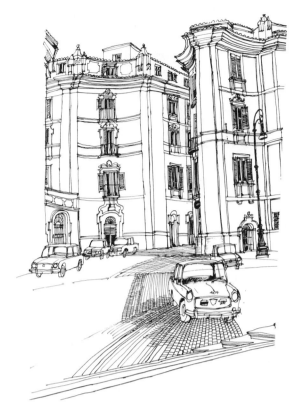

11.8 Handsome streets like this one in Pimlico, London, are often spoilt by parked cars. Streets and squares cease to be attractive or legible when filled with vehicles.

11.9 The relationship between streets and squares is often important. This composition of Baroque buildings in Rome contains narrow streets which open dramatically into a well-lit square.

begin, ensure the perspective is correctly handled, and make sure the marker on the route is prominently displayed.

Routes are not only deliberately landmarked, but undergo pleasant changes of direction or level. Frequently a curve in a street is the place to find a distinctive house or shopfront, and at changes of level there may be an old pub or group of ancient trees. Where steps occur they can enliven the scene especially if there are decorative handrails or lamps to light the way. Search out these incidental events, for they are part of the character of towns and are frequently being swept away or standardized by insensitive municipal authorities.

Towns with spatial richness consist of a mixture of the different sorts of streets listed earlier. Generally it is only the bigger cities and those with distinct historical layers, such as Edinburgh, York or Chester, that offer the full repertoire of types of routes situated close together. Other countries are more fortunate – around the Mediterranean it is commonplace to find in quite small places a network of fascinating streets and lanes leading to and from a town square. Here the spatial tensions experienced by the pedestrian are not only enhanced by

many changes of level, but by abrupt alterations of scale as, for instance, a grand central square suddenly opens into view. Added to this, the remnants of fortifications (as in Dubrovnik) provide a perimeter route around the town as well as attractive terminations to many of the alleyways.

Grand cities such as Paris, Washington or Turin contain wide tree-lined boulevards which are rather like linear squares. Here many different types of activity can be accommodated within the broad space of the street – pavement cafés, room for parking, tram routes, through traffic, central promenades and shaded areas for gossip. Largely the result of 19th-century highway engineering, the boulevard sought to bring beauty and ventilation to the heart of congested cities. Today they are worthy subjects for sketching as long as they are treated fairly broadly (the inclusion of too much detail would defeat the average artist).

For routes to uphold their civic responsibilities they should be legible places: streets need to be landmarked along their route and perhaps terminated at their ends. Yet the enjoyment of towns depends upon a balance between legibility and mystery. The narrow spaces of lanes and alleyways

11.10 *The curve of the main street in Holt, Norfolk, heightens the drama of entry to the town centre. The Georgian house to the right provides a welcome 'book-end' to the older houses and landmarks the end of the formal street.*

11.11 *The market square in Holt, Norfolk, has been partly invaded by subsequent building. The effect is to create an attractive sequence of spaces around the various buildings.*

provide mystery and spatial complexity to set against the right angles and open spaces of the major streets and squares. How the parts are put together is largely the result of history – towns normally represent their economic or cultural origins in the present layout of their streets. For the artist, a good street map, a willingness to explore on foot, and the use of the sketchbook as a tool for urban investigation are all equally important. Urban design is best taught in the field, by employing the freehand drawing to record and analyse. Our towns are a shared responsibility – their wellbeing is momentarily in our hands when we draw them. The much overlooked visual language of cities resides not only in what we can see and experience from the routes we take, but in how we elect to represent it and thereby protect it.

11.12 *The effect of height limits imposed by the Renaissance city fathers is evident in this sketch of Florence. The four-storey limit is further expressed by a unifying eaves overhang.*

Chapter 12

Landmarks, skyline and city image

Tall buildings, church spires and vertical features such as chimneys or pylons provide reference points to aid our navigation through towns. They are normally external landmarks in that we do not usually enter into them. In the city tall buildings rise above a basecourse of lower structures which comprise the everyday buildings – houses, warehouses, offices, and so on. For the landmarks to be read clearly they need to have background contrast so that they stand out from their neighbours. This means that landmarks are best set in an envelope of free space, and have a distinctive profile. Many towers in historic cities are so treated, especially the spires of churches or domes of town halls. The modern city poses a difficulty since the tall buildings are normally office blocks and they can look much like each other. So in many contemporary cities such as London or Birmingham one cannot navigate by the tall structures. Instead, one must search out the lower but more profiled and distinctive towers of earlier times to aid one's navigation.

Generally speaking, the basecourse of lower buildings is about four to six storeys high, and structures which rise significantly above this become 'landmarks'. Tall buildings can be 'dominant' structures – that is, they assert themselves through bulk – or 'prominent' structures which establish their presence through a distinctive profile or use of colour. Many modern office or residential blocks are 'dumb boxes' in visual terms since they fail to communicate a civic presence. A new generation of tall buildings is currently appearing on our city skylines (for instance, the AT&T Building in New York or Canary Wharf in London Docklands) which recognize their urban responsibilities. These structures are more profiled than their predecessors, especially at their tops.

If the success of a landmark depends upon its distinctiveness, or uniqueness, from its neighbours, then the designer can either manipulate the shape of the whole tower or (and this is cheaper) simply profile the top. Either way, uniqueness can be achieved and the skyline of the city enhanced. As we tend to view landmarks from within the city, the lower buildings obscure the bulk of the tower, thereby focusing our attention upon its top. Hence it may be legitimate only to shape the cap of the tower. Yet it should be also be borne in mind that from outside the city the whole landmark is visible, so that concentrating on the profile of the whole tower, and not just the top, becomes important (Manhattan viewed from across the water is a good example).

As landmarks compete for attention, there is some argument for treating skyscrapers as an

12.1 This street in Chicago is landmarked by towers of different generations (1930s and 1960s). The street becomes a showcase of architecture through the ages, each building vying for attention. With broad streets the skyline is particularly important.

12.2 This early 20th-century office tower in Vancouver rises above a base-course of more ordinary buildings. The curved roof provides a distinctive profile to the block.

12.3 Church towers (as here in northern France) provide frequent examples of how to shape, top and profile tall buildings.

12.4 At Siena Cathedral two forms of landmark have been employed – the tower and the dome. Each is set sufficiently apart to avoid competition. Here the tower acts as a useful marker to the square, alongside the cathedral.

12.5 *Old and new landmarks are here (in central Glasgow) set rather more in competition than co-operation with each other. Although a space has been formed to allow Alexander Thomson's church tower to rise unobscured, it remains bullied by the new neighbour.*

12.6 *The Seine in Paris is edged by handsome cliffs of apartment blocks and offices. The occasional church or university tower provides a useful point of reference to tourists and residents alike. Notice how the river has become a corridor for public display.*

ensemble. Skyline competition can enliven the urban scene, but it can also be beneficial to treat towers as a collection of related but different parts. When Sir Christopher Wren designed his 50 or so London churches after the Great Fire of 1666, he saw them as complementary elements both between themselves and with regard to the dominating presence of the dome of St Paul's. Each tower or spire was different, but taken together they had a certain unity.

The relationship between old and new city landmarks is a valuable subject for the sketchbook. It is best to draw the landmarks from within the street scene, showing their relationship to the urban context. Hence the sketch will probably contain streets as well as the tall buildings. By setting the

12.7 *Our appreciation of towns is usually derived from the public streets. Here in Carrington, Midlothian, the barn on the left deflects our view into the main street with the trees framing the entrance. The church tower acts as a useful landmark.*

landmarks into context, their importance as an aid to navigation becomes clearer. A sketch exploring the impact of one landmark upon another may dwell upon the need for singularity of form or the formal relationship of one skyscraper to another.

By understanding the relationship of different parts of the townscape – squares, streets, landmarks, etc. – one can begin to appreciate the inter-connected nature of urban design. Many modern cities are hard to find our way around because the routes are not landmarked, or because the tall buildings all look the same. Pedestrians experience abrupt changes of direction and level without any visual clues to guide them. Even motorists find themselves bewildered by a series of urban roads which sweep between near-identical buildings and

12.8 *High buildings which represent variations on a theme can be particularly satisfying. Here at Reepham in Norfolk two church towers complement each other without seeking to dominate the skyline.*

12.9 *The church spire not only landmarks the Bastide town of Eymet, but provides a local reference point from the market square. The offset side street is terminated by the church.*

across roundabouts each detailed in the same fashion as the one before. Tall buildings help us find our way around as long as each stands out from its neighbours. This is another reason why we should be cultivating architectural distinctiveness, not conformity, in tall buildings, and placing these 'unique' buildings at key points in the city.

As in much townscape analysis, the sketchbook is the best vehicle for cultivating an appreciation of the issues outlined above. The sketch does not have to be too literal, but it should seek to understand the language of the city. As towns are very complicated subjects to draw, one must be selective and edit out the unnecessary detail. If a drawing focuses upon skyline, then other elements in the view can be played down. And if a skyline feature is treated as an icon of the city (for example, Big Ben in London or the Eiffel Tower in Paris), then celebrate its presence with a bold rendition of it. There is a hierarchy in the skyline of most cities: representing the contrast between a central dominant structure and the supporting towers nearby can produce a sketch that is not only instructive but dramatic.

Gateways, entrances and doorways

The sense of arrival at places is important, and in recognition of this many cities and the buildings within them have elaborate gateways or doorways. Entry points are usually celebrated in this way except in the most utilitarian structures. At the other end of the scale, entry may consist only of a roundabout on a ring road or a collection of petrol stations marking an approach into a modern town. Historic towns, on the other hand, are normally well defined in terms of entry points, often because of the need for fortification in the past.

Entry points given celebration through architectural display are a common feature of European urban design. The grand gateways of Paris or Rome serve to define arrival at the city centre or the entry point into a special neighbourhood. Gateways into the city, into districts of the city,

13.1 The gateway into the old town of San Felice Circeo is marked by an abrupt change of direction. Once a fortified entrance, the gateway has only symbolic value today.

13.2 *This residential courtyard alongside a busy road in Holt, Norfolk, is marked by a pair of gatepiers and screen wall. The area is clearly identified as private territory, not public.*

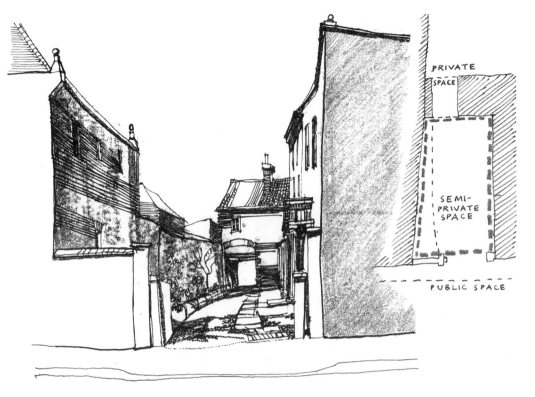

13.3 *This passageway through Sperlonga in Italy is divided into zones of territory by the presence of big overhead arches. The route becomes progressively private as one ascends.*

13.4 *Robert Adam's Pulteney Bridge provides an elegant river crossing and a gateway into the centre of Bath. Here the bridge is lined with shops which look outwards over the river.*

13.5 *The Ponte Vecchio in Florence also acts as a gateway into the city and a shopping street. Space is provided for stall holders beneath the arches of this handsome structure.*

and then into public buildings establish a legible hierarchy. In similar fashion entrance doorways into private houses often lead to lesser doorways within the interior. A sense of hierarchy between outside and hallway, then between hallway and living rooms, and living rooms and kitchens are part of the everyday language of domestic design. The same should apply to the city.

Modern gateways are rare, though the need for crime prevention through territorial definition and surveillance of entrances has led to their revival of late. Such gateways into private housing estates or industrial parks serve both functional and decorative needs. They define entrances into distinctive domains in much the same way that gateways in historic towns give expression to the privacy or security needs of different groups or classes of people.

13.6 *The Doric porticoes to this imposing crescent of houses in Glasgow define entrances and provide a rhythm to the wider composition. By linking together entrances the porticoes have a scale in keeping with the crescent.*

Gateways and doorways are rewarding subjects to draw. As they define routes into and out of places, they provide a visual tension which derives from a well-engineered constriction at a certain point. Often a narrowing of the route is supplemented by a change of direction or level. The materials of the road surface might also change at critical points, and there may be windows or arrow slots overlooking the space. Such gateways do not only occur at the edges of towns but at the entrance to distinctive neighbourhoods within them. In Oxford, for instance, the gateways to many of the colleges are so treated, as are the palace grounds in princely cities such as St Petersburg or Prague. A modern trend is to define neighbourhoods of the city by such means, as witnessed by the Chinese gateway in London's Soho. Here the urban designer has the challenge of selecting an appropriate entrance, and giving it definition through symbolic structures at the edge (as in Piazza Del Popolo in Rome) or in the centre of the space (as in the former Euston Arch in London).

Most gateways derive their justification from questions of security, but they also perform a useful function in terms of legibility. Big cities are perceived as collections of villages or neighbourhoods. Each should have its own community focus, public buildings and entrances. The edge of the 'village' is often defined by a major road or railway line with entrances marked by significant buildings. Often, as in the approaches into Hampstead Garden Suburb, London, the entrance buildings look like gateways and suggest an element of celebration. Hence to draw them is not only enjoyable but instructive of the nature of cities.

The modern movement in architecture and town planning played down the question of entrances. The wish to depict an air of democracy and freedom led to openness, not enclosure, in urban design. As a consequence, the 20th-century city became windswept in appearance, with spaces between buildings lacking territorial definition and used mainly for low-grade activities such as car parking. The re-creation of boundary, edge and gateway is one of the challenges faced by current urban designers. Modern cities are undergoing a crisis of legibility which the introduction of gateways, using perhaps the roundabouts on the inner ring roads as a starting point, would help to solve.

The perception and definition of 'place', from the regional scale to the domestic, is of crucial importance to design. A regional identity bred of cultural, geographic and social factors will lead to a Europe of variety and pluralism, as against monotony and standardization. In this, gateways and boundaries are important. Between England and Scotland on the M74 there is no customs point, but a stone wall and piers on either side of the motorway proclaims the entrance to Scotland. This gateway is purely symbolic – it makes manifest

a desire for national identity. One could argue that Dover is a gateway to Britain, with the white cliffs performing a similar iconographic function as the walls and piers across the motorway north of Carlisle. Seen in this way, Dover is an entry point establishing the first taste of Englishness for many people. The town is, therefore, setting standards of culture and design for the whole country and should be designed as an entrance way rather than simply as a seaside town.

Many engineering structures serve secondary functions as gateways into cities. The Humber Bridge is a gateway into Hull, as is Robert Adam's Pulteney Bridge into the centre of Bath. Gateways, therefore, come in many forms and not all are conventionally designed as entrance porticoes. Bridge engineers increasingly see their structures as entrance points and design them in a fashion which celebrates arrival.

A gateway is best regarded as a deliberate break within a city wall or the careful marking of a boundary of territory. It is important to draw both the boundary and the break for each is supporting the same purpose. Sometimes the boundary is clear, as with medieval fortifications, but often the territorial edge is not so well defined, and you may have to use your imagination to see the architecture as gateway markers. For instance, an urban fringe may be marked by a line of bungalows and the point of entry by a pair of car showrooms facing each other across a main road.

Within the town, entry points exist though they may not be immediately apparent. A roundabout or exit ramp from a motorway may serve as an entrance gateway with perhaps a tall building marking its presence. Again, the artist must employ some insight and imagination to see these as modern gateways. Having sketched such a scene, it is easier to imagine a cluster of buildings making an urban gateway – you can move from description of the present situation to proposing some future change.

Lesser gateways in a town are quite common. Many modern shopping centres employ expressive portals in order to announce the position of

13.7 *Gatepiers are often part of the dec- orative tradition of older areas. These splendid gatepiers from a middle-class suburb in Glasgow both define the edge of private territory and enrich the public realm.*

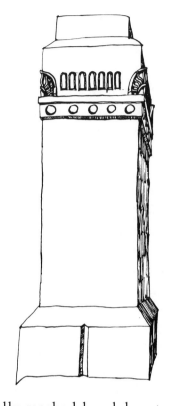

entrances to malls or car parks. The language of entrance and advertising is often skilfully exploited in such areas. In historic towns the gateways into cathedral closes or market squares are sometimes given civic expression, and deserve sketchbook analysis. In much the same fashion large buildings have imposing entrances which tell you immediately where the main doors are located. Town halls, Victorian railway stations and court houses all employ a simple language of entrance definition usually incorporating columns and pediments. By way of contrast, modern buildings (especially those of the 1960s and 1970s) often fail to mark their entrance, so that, for example, to find the doors to the Sainsbury Centre at the University of East Anglia is an unwelcome trial.

Expressed entrances frequently open on to interesting interior hallways which lead the visitor to secondary doorways and corridors. The progression through from street, to entrance, to interior is peri-

odically marked by elaborate doorways. The sketchbook study could focus upon the processional route and its punctuation, or upon the details of the portals or doorways. If the latter path is followed, the door furniture and aspects of craftsmanship could be highlighted.

Doors and doorcases are difficult subjects to draw. It is worth spending time on them as they often represent a greater amount of architectural investment than much of the remainder of the building. Georgian doorways are particularly complex subjects, but at least ensure, when you are sketching them, that the proportions are correct, for this is what probably most concerned the original designer. In your drawing you can simplify the decorative carvings or simply record one section of detail, but the proportions of width to height of the door and of any panels should be depicted as accurately as possible.

Many doorways or portals contain the coats of

arms or inscriptions of their benefactors. The presence of such embellishment simply highlights the symbolic importance of doorways or gateways. Much recent design has sought to resurrect the language of the doorway and to revive its spiritual importance. In terms of building design, much has been achieved in the past ten years, but in the context of the town or countryside as a whole, the idea of gateways has not received as much attention.

If the culture of Europe resides in her distinctive cities as against countries, then doorways, gateways and entrances are very much part of local and regional character. In Barcelona, for instance, the approach to the design of entrances is quite different to that employed in Glasgow – the Catalan tradition is far removed from the Celtic one. To maintain these differences, not just between cities but

within them, the freehand sketch is a vital means of recording, understanding and cultivating a climate for preserving local idiosyncrasies.

A good exercise is to search out entrances at the various scales – urban, district, neighbourhood, building, interior, etc. Each can be recorded and related to the other in the form of a network or in terms of spatial hierarchy. By relating the scale of the doorway to its sphere of perceptual influence, one can begin to understand the language of cities and where the visual clues become disjointed. Cities encompass patterns of behaviour and networks of design, with doorways providing the links between one system and another. Hence, of all the architectural elements, few have more symbolic value than the doorway or portal.

Chapter 14

The façades of buildings

Like an honest face, the elevations of a building should tell you something about what function it serves, how it is built, and when it was constructed. In addition, the degree of embellishment or grandeur probably provides clues to the civic importance of the building. By drawing the façade of a building, you will gain insights into the intentions of the architect and his or her aspirations as an urban designer. Additionally, you will probably understand better the role of the building within the social or economic structure of the area,

14.1 *This Edwardian office building in central Glasgow tells you that the public functions are to be found on the ground floor with the entrance well marked. Above is found repetitive office space.*

the reason for employing a distinctive style or pattern of architecture, or the justification for adopting a particular mode of technology.

Your freehand sketch is, therefore, both graphic description and historical analysis. Generally speaking, historic buildings are more complex structures than modern ones, partly as a result of layers of change which have left their mark on the elevations, but mainly because they do not subscribe to the simplified abstraction of contemporary buildings. In the past the role of a building may have been to decorate a street, terminate a vista or provide a supporting role to a public monument. Today buildings are more likely to express their structural prowess, or their use of a sophisticated cladding system. Whichever expression is sought by the modern architect, it is unlikely to relate directly to wider civic ambitions.

Drawing the architectural façade may highlight some aspect of current or historical theory of design, or the sketch may simply tell you about the social pattern of living at a particular place or time. The main point is to get beyond the surface of the drawing into an analysis of social and technological factors or of design theory. Whether you choose to sketch a city or country building, a private house or public monument, a modern structure or ancient one, the same general rules should apply.

By drawing the façade of a building, you are focusing your attention upon the principal area for expression exploited by architect and engineer alike. The method of expression may be obvious – perhaps by the use of exposed columns; or more subtly – perhaps by the skilful adoption of proportional harmonies. Remember that, though the designer of a building may seek to link the exterior expression to the interior pattern of spaces and functions, he or she is mainly concerned with how the building looks from the outside. The yardstick by which to judge architectural quality is primarily that of the elevations.

14.2 The designer of this small cinema in Ukiah, California, gives expression to the tower and canopy in a fashion typical of the 1930s. The tower acts as a hinge around which the rest of the design pivots. The bottle-cap shape of the top of the tower alludes perhaps to the café found inside.

CLUES TO INTERNAL FUNCTION

Many buildings employ a visual code based upon making manifest the function of the building through elevational expression. The clues are both direct and indirect. With old industrial buildings, and some modern ones, the presence of cranes, lifting hoists and large door openings announce the presence of a warehouse. The office block may betray its function through the use of repeating grids of windows, strip lighting visible through large sheets of glass, and the lack of curtains or blinds. Likewise a modern block of flats will perhaps have expressed balconies which provide 'gardens in the air', different window sizes, and security systems around the main entrance. Designers wishing to exploit the functional clues may link the balconies into bands 20 or so storeys high, or raise the block of flats on stilts to provide space at the ground for common facilities such as laundries or shops. In the case of office blocks, the architect may allow the entrance to project forwards with a canopy for signage, or change the grid of windows where conference facilities or staff refreshment areas are located. In this way there are clues to both the function of the building and to that of its various parts.

Many people interpret these visual codes when deciding what the functions are within a particular building. We are all familiar with the traditional use of columns to mark an entrance to a public building, the use of a rotunda to denote a space of importance inside or an atrium marking a gathering space within the building. This simple language of expression can be found in provincial court houses as well as in many modern office buildings in business parks. On a more mundane level, a single-storey structure with high-level bands of windows denotes accommodation for utility companies or perhaps public toilets. These buildings do not require signs: their appearance tells most people what goes on inside.

A recent trend in architecture has been to enliven the façades of dull buildings such as offices by exaggerating on the outside the differences in internal function. Many modern office blocks contain atria to help with both the control of the internal environment and provide space for informal staff meetings. By bringing the atrium to the outside, the elevations offer a play of solid against void. In addition, as the atrium often contains an abundance of trees and shrubs, it can appear as if an area of garden had been trapped inside the building 'envelope'. Assuming clear glass has been employed, the outside observer can see into the office building, so that not only the elevations are enlivened, but internal activities are relayed to the street outside. Moreover, if the building entrance leads through the atrium, a lightweight canopy may project forwards, thereby enriching further the building's façade. By such means, dull architectural subjects can be made interesting, and monotonous façades more lively.

The more that internal functions are allowed to express themselves externally, the richer become the elevations. The classical language of entrance portico, colonnade, rotunda and dome gave expression not just to different structural members or constructional systems, but to the internal activities or functions of a particular building. The façade of a classical or neoclassical building is not a flat plane, but a series of layers of connected structural or decorative parts. Added to this, the interest in pure geometry of the neoclassicists led to an architecture consisting of cubes, circles, semicircles and triangles. Hence an abstract language of shapes forming the structure of a building was counterbalanced by surface decoration which often denoted the functions housed. A typical building of the period was broken down into parts, with each serving a different function and given a separate form of expression. In addition, the public was in many cases allowed to penetrate part of the edge of the building before reaching the main entrance. A transition space for meeting friends or colleagues was therefore provided, often within the thickness of the wall or within the depth of a projecting porch or recessed entrance. Elevational richness thus derived from a consideration of how people

behaved when moving from the outside to the inside of a building.

The cinema is one of the more interesting building types of the 20th century. It gives expression to its function as a building for public gatherings; it makes its presence felt by a dramatic tower or exterior sign, the roof of the auditorium rises above the surrounding rooftops; and the entrance, foyer and bars are often separately expressed. As buildings, cinemas are easily recognized and rarely confused with their sister building – the theatre. Since cinemas require few windows, designers have traditionally concentrated instead on the manipulation of mass and surface decoration. Brickwork is often arranged in panels, allowing a tension to be created between the juxtaposition of horizontal and vertical lines. Entrances are light and airy and contrast pleasantly with the solid auditoria. In sketching such buildings the artist should dwell upon these points in order to learn about the design of cinemas through the process of drawing.

CLUES TO STRUCTURAL SYSTEMS

It is a modernist maxim that buildings should give expression to their means of construction. A search for authenticity in architecture marks much of the 20th century. The trouble is that to express nothing but the structure of a building can lead to rather dull architecture.

14.3 Hill House by Mackintosh does not have a principal front. The design grows naturally from the plan with living rooms, master bedroom and staircase clearly expressed on the outside.

14.4 *The façade of this Renaissance church in Gaeta, Italy, creates a grand impression to a city square. The architect has concentrated on the front rather than on the whole building.*

Freehand drawing is a handy means of understanding structure. Victorian architects such as Richard Norman Shaw used the sketch to record the skills of medieval carpenters or the method employed in framing church roofs. Today you can use the freehand drawing to analyse the steelwork of modern structures such as Sir Norman Foster's tree-like roof trusses at Stansted Airport, or the concrete framing of a modern grain silo.

Many modern architects are more at home giving expression to structure than to function. This is partly because the use of a building changes fairly quickly over time and hence to make functional expression the main aim of the design can make a nonsense of a building in the longer term. But the main reason is that modern technology has made 20th-century buildings more exciting structurally than in any other way. Hence designers such as Renzo Piano or Michael Hopkins concentrate on structural daring in preference to proportional harmony or the expression of a building's programme. It is often a case of constructional invention being linked to new ways of servicing buildings, with the result that our current 'green' awareness finds expression in buildings with solar screens, stepped sections and exposed movable louvres.

There are three broad ways of constructing a building: by frame, by load-bearing wall, and by self-supporting panel. Framed structures probably pre-date the others simply because of the wide availability of building timber in the ancient forests of the temperate world. Load-bearing brickwork was introduced into Britain by the Romans and began to become commonplace as timber became scarce in the late Middle Ages. Large-panel construction is chiefly a 20th-century invention and has the benefit that it can be prefabricated and speedily erected. As the panels are load-bearing, the walls provide both enclosure and structure within the same unit and this leads to obvious economies, though often at the price of aesthetics.

This simple classification of constructional systems can be enlarged to include suspended structures where the tensile rather than compressive strength of materials is exploited. A mixture of structural systems is frequently represented on the same elevation of a building, thereby adding to the complexity of the façade. For example, the Mound Stand by Hopkins at the Lords Cricket Ground uses load-bearing brickwork and stretched lightweight fabric canopies to good effect.

14.5 *The Barcelona Pavilion by Mies van der Rohe seeks to occupy the space around its edge by wings of structure and overhanging roofs. The building, pool and paving area are united by a consistency of approach.*

The degree to which the structural system employed is made visible determines the appearance of the building. A concrete-framed office can have its basic structure disguised by a glass cladding system which gives no expression at all to the framing members. Alternatively, the structure can be expressed, giving an otherwise bland façade a sense of interest or organization in visual terms. A well-expressed series of columns and beams can absorb the visual chaos of the modern apartment block, as exemplified by some of the poorer areas of downtown Hong Kong. Your sketch can draw attention to the frame by highlighting its presence through shadows, or play it down in order to express some other aspect of the building. Frequently the use of an exposed frame gives expression to both the structural and functional logic of a building. Sir Giles Gilbert Scott's London power stations make manifest both the method of construction and the internal arrangements of complex, yet publicly visible, buildings. Although your sketch may focus upon the main structures alone, it is hard to overlook the architectural drama given by Scott to the generators or chimneys.

Load-bearing walls can be treated so that every brick, or block of masonry, is expressed, or designed so that the wall reads as a single panel of construction. From afar, large areas of brickwork can appear to be seamless wall planes rather than composed of individual units, but different colours of brick are often employed to create patterns on a larger scale. Where bricks are mixed with stone, the relative scale of the parts of the wall can establish lines of tension which 18th-century designers used to define edges and create visual frames. In many cases you will find that the whole façade of a brick building is trimmed in stone in order to create a 'picture-frame' around the house.

The wall and its framing members are essential to the rhythm of a façade. Frequently the structural members become the main means of decorating a building. The classical orders established rules whereby embellishment subscribed to a predetermined plan. Often the orders obscured rather than

14.6 *The Pompidou Centre by Piano and Rogers makes dramatic expression of structure, building services and movement systems. The old idea of a building façade has been turned literally inside out in this building.*

expressed the structural logic of a building – and it was partly an escape from the limitations of the classical decorative language that justified the flight into the Gothic Revival and thence, a century later, into modern architecture.

It is rewarding to compare an architect-designed building of the 18th century to that erected by an engineer or surveyor. The design of a country house or town hall of the time would no doubt be correct from an academic point of view, but one would be hard pressed to identify clearly what method of construction had been employed. By way of contrast, an area of dockland would contain wharfs and warehouses of honest construction and simple, unadorned lines. The hand of the engineer would be evident in the use of robust arches, plain areas of undecorated brickwork and functionally expressed beams or roof trusses. In both cases the façade makes visible the values that led to the erection of the building – values which the act of drawing should reveal.

Whether you are drawing for pleasure or discovery, the architectural sketch is best rendered in good light – preferably sunlight. The texture of the various building materials, the play of structure against background walling, the depth of windows and façade projections are better observed in strong light, and best depicted with the aid of shadows.

14.7 *In this drawing of a section of the west façade of St Mark's in Venice, the structural logic of arches and columns is not obscured by lavish decoration. Embellishment here consists of reinforcing the logic of the structure by sculpture and friezes.*

14.8 *The varied activities in this harbourside development in Gaeta, Italy, are expressed in extensions to the main building and in the form of cheerful signs.*

As in plan drawing, shadows or shading can enhance the three-dimensional qualities and bring alive qualities of the façade which have become obscured by generations of soot deposits or by your own overfamiliarity with such buildings. The architectural sketch is a means of cultivating a personal sensitivity to buildings and to their construction. Whether your subject is a vernacular house, a modern factory or historic church, the sketch should make visible to yourself some of the key qualities of the architectural design.

CLUES TO PROPORTIONAL SYSTEMS

If you see the elevations of a building in more geometric terms, it may become evident that the design is based upon a proportional system of one kind or another. Many buildings of classical inspiration employ proportional harmonies based upon squares, circles and the golden section. Beauty was seen to lie in the adoption of shapes and outlines which related well to each other and which contained in themselves a harmonic repose. Hence the front of a house may be a double square on its side with windows also in the proportion of a double square placed vertically. Sometimes an elevation may consist of a circle within a square or the placing and size of windows may be dictated by the diagonal lines of the golden section.

In modern buildings the repeating pattern of lines within curtain walling may also subscribe to similar rules of proportion. At South Quay Plaza on the Isle of Dogs in London Docklands, an office development by Seifert Architects mixes double squares, squares and diamonds to good effect. Here the buildings can be viewed across the river Thames, allowing the calculated use of harmonic subdivisions to have maximum impact on the observer.

Often architects draw attention to the key lines which they want you to read in order to understand the proportional system they are using. String courses may be employed or the building may be set upon a solid base (*piano nobile*). Frequently corner definition is employed, thereby creating a rectangular frame across the façade. By changing the colour, texture, or the nature of the constructional material, the designer is able to express the critical lines or planes of the proportional system.

The problem that architects often face is how to subdivide a large elevation into smaller parts which

14.9 *The brute force of shuttered concrete is well expressed in these buildings on London's South Bank. The style known as Brutalism sought to exaggerate the scale of construction and the visual possibilities of concrete left in its natural state.*

14.10 These buildings in Chicago exploit not just the technical possibilities of steel construction, but the aesthetic ones as well. The contrast between the stone-clad skyscraper and the one finished in glass is immediately evident. Open public spaces like this demand a matching architecture of scale and interest.

fix the position of windows, doors, columns, etc. in a logical fashion. A proportional system should embrace both large and small parts, and should also allow the observer to 'read' where the important elements or functions are located. Many modern buildings are so abstract in design that the same pattern is wrapped around all sides of a building irrespective of functional hierarchy. On the other hand, a study of older buildings, even functional ones like warehouses, can reveal the use of proportional systems worked out to a surprising level of detail, if you can be bothered to uncover them.

SOURCES OF DECORATION

A modern abstract façade can add up to dull architecture. Similarly a severe historical building whose beauty derives almost totally from proportional systems tends not to attract our attention for very long. Just as a townscape made up almost entirely of modern office blocks can be a visually depressing experience, so too a district of buildings constructed according to strict classical principles can be quite lifeless. The Victorian writer on art John Ruskin was particularly critical of Queen Street in the heart of Georgian Edinburgh for this very reason when he visited the city in 1853.

It is a responsibility of buildings that they enrich the public domain. Frequently the sources of richness derive from the simple expression of how peo-

ple wish to live. For example, an apartment block will probably contain balconies where families can sit in the sun, dry their clothes or grow their plants. These activities not only enrich the façade, but provide justification for the presence of certain architectural details: the balcony may be edged by a balustrade or a colourful awning may protect the area from the midday sun. Similarly French windows can add an extra dimension to a room by opening up a view on to the street, but because such large openings require closing at night for acoustic and visual reasons, there may be window shutters as well as doors and probably a lace curtain. All three features become part of the architecture of the façade – and worthy subjects for drawing.

Entrance doors are often similarly treated, and where there is a slight change of level, plants around the steps add to the diversity of the scene. As doorways require to be lit, there are often interesting light fittings which project from the wall face and complement the other special qualities of the entrance.

Each element of the building can be so treated. The celebration of function in this everyday fashion is part of our architectural tradition. The more the façade gives expression to the activities of the building, the richer the architecture. Earlier we saw how the form of the building can be manipulated to allow people to 'read' the activities it contains, but here the detailed expression of function is the source of our interest.

Shops are a good example of how local colour can be provided at the base of buildings. Not only will the form of the building change to accommodate a different function, but there will be shop signs, goods on display and pavement activity to add diversity to the immediate environment. Where shops, banks and restaurants occur, there will probably be competition for space and attention, and here the architecture will probably respond. This visual richness bred of competition is a healthy aspect of the building façades of most high streets.

Decorative ironwork, applied columns, pilasters

14.11 These drawings of Georgian terraces in Glasgow show how proportional systems can create elevation with repose and dignity.

and banners are other ingredients of elevational embellishment. Often the orthodox will be distorted in order to attract attention: exaggerated columns may mark a shop or supermarket front, or ironwork may be twisted into the curving forms of Art Nouveau.

By focusing upon the decorative elements of the building façade, the student or artist will be able to relate embellishment to function. Pure decoration in architecture can become a sham unless it is justified by use or legibility. Although decoration is eminently drawable, the real benefit lies in relating the four main strands together – of linking structure, function, proportion and decoration into a united whole. Buildings are complex entities, and though a specific style or artistic movement may focus upon a particular aspect of their construction, most façades reflect a compromise between conflicting priorities. The freehand drawing can help break down the façade into its component parts, and in the process provide insights into the nature of architectural design.

14.12 *South Quay Plaza on the Isle of Dogs seeks to apply proportional systems to give expression to a modern office block.*

14.13 *Buildings at angled corners are often given special treatment. Here at the Russell Institute in Paisley the façade rhythms reach a climax in a dramatic entrance tower topped by an Art Deco angel. Such buildings should be sought out and cherished. Note the classical subdivision overlaid by modernist principles.*

Machinery and the functional tradition

The functional character of trains, machinery and ships makes a pleasant contrast to the historicism or concern for applied style in buildings, especially very recent ones. Machinery makes no concession to surface aesthetics, and derives its visual qualities instead from meeting strict utilitarian criteria: rivets are left exposed and moving parts placed on the outside for ease of access and servicing. The result of this unassuming functionalism is often to produce objects of rare beauty or structures of haunting presence. To draw them is to understand their essence as working objects and to appreciate their form. When placed against everyday buildings and landscapes, the industrial object has both an immediacy and charm which can be attractive to draw.

Sketching machinery is not easy, yet the functionalism of the subject often gives the picture great power. The 'functional aesthetic' is normally expressed at both a detailed level (in the bolts, welds and pressed metal panels) and in the general massing or arrangement of the subject. You have only to look at such essentials as the steps up to the cabs of diesel engines or the door handles of tractors, to realize that a rugged utilitarianism reigns. If beauty is to be found in the machine-made detail, the same is true of these objects as seen in their entirety. Their silhouettes are often evocative, and the exposed frames of such structures as pit heads and gantry cranes makes them striking features in any landscape.

Industrial landscapes are often linear affairs. The parallel lines of railway tracks or dock basins allow the artist to exploit the directness of single-point perspective. The balance between horizontal and vertical lines is also important. Since trees are often lacking from such places or appear only as a self-seeded scrub, the lines of the industrial features are not generally softened by landscape. Hence the artist can approach the subject using 6B pencils and plenty of dark wash or crayon. The spirit of such places lends them to bold representation.

It is often a good idea to exploit silhouette, especially in structures which are quite high. Industrial buildings and working machinery are not normally painted – their colour derives from oily splashes, rusting steelwork and the hues of manufacture. In a landscape of flour mills and cement works much will look frosted by the white dust, and mining areas will be darkened by the colour of coal and iron ore. Such places tend to be dark and rather dramatic, with 'spillage' providing a counterbalance to sculptural shape. The best industrial scenes are almost sublime (to paraphrase the 18th-century

15.1 *Utilitarian structures such as these Thameside warehouses in London offer compositional lessons to designers.*

Romantic Edmund Burke) in their honest juxtaposition of structure, dilapidation and enormous scale.

Graphics frequently play an important role within the functional landscape. The numbering of railway wagons and the alphabetic coding of buildings adds a further component to the air of rationalism. The graphic style is necessarily practical – a form of squared-off lettering tends to be used, often in conjunction with exaggerated scale. The scene (and hence the analytical sketch) can take on the qualities of a Russian Constructivist painting as a result of the almost abstract superimposition of graphics, structures and architecture.

As the lettering does not normally have to appeal to city sensibilities, it is often crudely painted or at least has a visual carefreeness typical of industrial landscapes. In modern factory areas, the graphics are often part of corporate identity (as with British Steel) and have a corresponding lifelessness, but in older industrial areas the style of lettering can be rather idiosyncratic and hence more rewarding for the artist.

The sketches which result from a close scrutiny of industrial areas can have artistic value, as well as helping to teach us lessons about design. If buildings are designed purely out of practical considerations, with no special regard for appearance, then the resulting structures have a form quite different from buildings designed on aesthetic grounds. Only the 'high tech' modernists such as Sir Richard Rogers and Sir Norman Foster produce contemporary architecture that has qualities which derive from the spirit of our industrial tradition. These architects place the building services on the outside and leave cranes on the roof to suggest a flexible and utilitarian approach to design. Their use of sheet metal and an exposed, often exaggerated, structure has obvious parallels with buildings associated with the manufacturing process. The Lloyds Building in London is a *tour de force* of such an approach to design, though to this author it is as unhappy in the City of London as a factory would be. But to understand some of the more assertive aspects of contemporary architecture, a few days

15.2 *Coal mines (here at Chislet Colliery in Kent) can be a collection of bold abstract shapes grouped into sculptural assemblies in open landscapes. They too offer lessons in architectural composition and construction.*

15.3 *An understanding of perspective and structure is important if subjects such as this coal-loading area at Snowdown Colliery in Kent are to be attempted. Notice how steel construction unifies both the railway wagons and the colliery structure.*

spent sketching decaying pit heads at local coal mines or dilapidated warehouses at the dockside should prove invaluable.

The current fashion for a kind of fragmented modernism (known as Deconstructivism) has part of its origins in the architecture of industrial areas. The peeling away of façade to expose the structure, the distortions of scale and angle, and the expression of physical change or structural impermanence are qualities frequently encountered in factory areas or mechanical plant. When decay has set in, these monuments to functionalism can be romantic in the extreme, but they can also teach us much about the role of frame, panel, fixing and assembly. In analysing such subjects through the sketchbook, we can gain an invaluable insight into the

15.4 *These sketches of Santiaga Calatrava's bridge at Bach de Roda in Barcelona seek to capture this engineer's extraordinary grasp of geometry and form. Such structures can uplift the spirit in inner-city areas.*

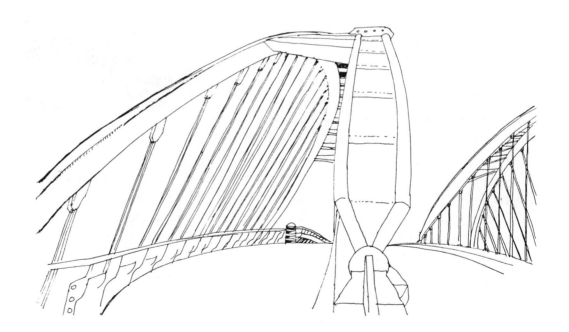

construction of industrial architecture and machinery.

Nature, when it encroaches, has an interesting relationship with the industrial landscape. Trees are rarely planted as decorative elements – they simply seed themselves in odd corners or high up on the outsides of buildings. Wild flowers and creepers are also quick to colonize waste areas and these can provide an attractive foil to the straight lines of factory buildings. Try not to ignore the presence of nature – the odd weed or sprouting willow can add a welcome air of tranquillity or contradiction to the sketch. Nature is also good at giving a sense of scale to the drawing. A typical industrial scene has an inhuman scale and though this is one of the charms of the subject, a few weeds (and even the occasional factory worker) will immediately establish the size of what has been drawn. The contrast in scale and texture between the built and natural elements makes not only attractive sketches, but is instructive of the connected role of townscape and landscape within our cities.

While buildings and cities are densely inhabited, many industrial scenes appear unpopulated. Instead fork-lift trucks, lorries and railway wagons tend to occupy the spaces between buildings. Since they are important elements in most of our functional landscapes, their presence cannot be ignored. In many cases the style of the structures is reflected in the design or detail of the means of transport. Hence in dockland areas the wharves and cranes have features in common with the ships, and in factories the conveyor belts share a visual language with aspects of the buildings.

Sketching the structure of the industrial landscape has arguably more lessons to teach the designer of buildings or objects than more conventional architectural subjects. The lessons are best learnt through the sketchbook, but in addition the drawings themselves can be of great power and interest.

15.5 *The character of the industrial landscape extends not just through buildings but the spaces between them. Here at Kalamazoo in Michigan, railway tracks, traffic signs, trains and telegraph poles establish an appropriate foreground to the factories.*

15.6 *This Russian-built bulldozer contains details and forms which could be translated into an architectural context.*

116

15.7 *Railway architecture (as at this station in Ukiah, California) offers designers many useful references, both in the buildings, machinery and track equipment.*

Chapter 16

Landscape

The landscape of cities and the countryside around them can be divided roughly into the following categories:

- tree-planted squares and parks;
- waste land occupied by vegetation;
- trees used for visual screening such as around industrial estates;
- mature parkland in the countryside;
- private gardens and courtyards.

These various landscape types can each be sketched and their aesthetic qualities explored. Before doing so, however, it is important to under- stand the structure of landscape and how best to represent its basic ingredients – hills, fields, bound- aries, hedges, paving, etc.

Landscape drawing is a well-developed art, and sufficient guidance in its principles is given else- where to save duplication here. As a rule, the artist should concentrate upon the structure and form of landscape, leaving matters of detail to a secondary sketch. The character of towns requires an appreci- ation of landscape, but vegetation is rarely a domi- nant element in the scene. Normally the structure of land form, the pattern of landscape, and the geometry of planting are the essential ingredients. As landscape and architecture are closely inter-

16.1 *Landscape pro- vides the setting for most towns. The open fields of Norfolk and remnants of old hedgerows enhance the scene of the market town of Reepham. The church towers built on high ground make distant landmarks and provide the focus for the drawing.*

16.2 Perspective plays a large part in landscape drawing. This view of a water works outside Glasgow exploits the strange geometries of such places.

woven within towns and the city edge, the principles already mentioned for drawing the urban elements can be applied to the natural ones.

Hence seek out patterns and structures within the landscape as you would with the buildings and represent them broadly. See the trees and hedges as enclosing 'rooms', as brick walls do in the urban scene. Tall trees, especially if columnar in shape, can be depicted as landmarks rising above the background townscape. In Continental cities the spires of churches are often set in competition with the cypresses planted in the nearby graveyards. Similarly, the parallel lines of trees planted along a city street can have a formality nearly as great as that of the enclosing buildings. The perceptive eye of the artist should pick out these qualities of form and geometry, and represent them clearly in the sketch.

The modern landscape often contains straight lines and bold arrangements. The urban fringe is frequently filled with large-scale engineering structures which contrast with the old cottages and farmsteads of former times. Modern by-passes, electricity pylons and reservoir dams often stand right at the edge of the city. The difference in scale and the strict geometry of the new structures are worthy of a well-aimed sketch. The new landscapes of

the 20th century are crowded into the green belts around most cities. Their modernist lines, smooth surfaces and strictly controlled vegetation contrast pleasantly with the landscapes of earlier generations.

The modern landscapes of reservoirs, airfields and science parks can all be explored, understood and enjoyed through freehand sketching. The scale and speed of modern life is well captured in the new landscapes of the urban edge. As in much townscape drawing, an understanding of perspective is important, especially as many characteristic landscapes of the 20th century are made up of parallel lines. Straight field edges, railway and electricity lines, the geometric pattern of modern forestry, all require a good grasp of perspective if they are to be accurately represented.

These parallel landscapes often overlap older field boundaries or the ancient alignment of a country lane. Hence the modern elements can be drawn alongside an earlier order, making not only an interesting drawing, but highlighting the historical processes which shape our landscape. The patterns of different geometrics, of old and new textures, frequently extend through both urban and rural areas. Compared to the countryside well away from towns, the landscapes at the urban edge are

16.3 *Landscape and engineering are the two main elements of modern road design. Here at the Edinburgh city by-pass electricity pylons form a barrier between the road and Pentland Hills and reinforce the geometrics of the road system.*

16.4 *The bold patterns of the ploughed fields in upland landscapes can make for interesting drawings. The flowing lines of hills, fields and shelter belts stand in contrast to the more man-made landscapes of the urban fringe (see figure 16.1).*

16.5 *Invading vegetation tends to soften older industrial landscapes. This mining village in Midlothian has long ceased to be a working community and has now taken on the quality of an open-air museum amidst lush vegetation.*

16.6 *In suburban areas landscape design and architectural design are often well balanced. Different shapes and colours of trees complement the diverse patterns of building in this drive in Glasgow.*

16.7 *The proximity of the date palm to this merchant's house in Palma, Marjorca, creates a tension between building and landscape design. The terrace provides an opportunity to enjoy the shade of the tree and gives privacy to the main apartments on the first floor.*

16.8 *The density of planting along this road in Glasgow results in the landscape elements dominating the urban ones. The different textures of the trees and plants have been deliberately exploited partly to aid identifying the species involved.*

complex subjects, being neither truly rural nor truly urban. They are the servicing areas for the city, and therefore contain sewage farms, railway yards, industrial parks and motorway corridors interspersed with remnants of the older farmed landscape. The somewhat artificial boundary between town and country is represented in the untidy and often vandalized countryside immediately around cities. Using the sketchbook in these areas can result in interesting compositions. The challenging material of the urban countryside is also helpful in teaching landscape design and in cultivating an appreciation of issues facing modern geographers and town planners.

The modern industrial landscape at the urban edge frequently contains relics of the Industrial Revolution. In former mining areas heaps of coal spoil, like mini mountains, can be found often alongside the dilapidated remains of pit winding gear. These relics have a poetic quality, especially if softened by invading vegetation. Disused canals and railway lines have a similar quality, and in time, perhaps the elements of the 20th-century landscape (pylons, motorways) will also be transformed into romantic ruins.

The pre-industrial landscape made up primarily of agricultural countryside and compact settlements has given way to dispersed towns and disrupted countryside. As a consequence, the town now extends into the countryside, leaving pockets of fields and orchards marooned in the city. Hence fragments of the countryside can often be found in towns, and transplants of the city in the countryside (frequently in the form of the new towns or business parks). The old rigid distinction between town and countryside has been broken, creating much material for exploration through the sketchbook.

Green belts seek to hold on to the romantic notion of the countryside surviving as a discrete entity alongside towns. They are usually well-defined areas consisting of country parks, old planted estates and modern recreation facilities. They provide good material and a tranquil setting for those wishing to learn through freehand drawing.

Landscape sketches are more successful if there is

16.9 *These palm trees in a courtyard in Palma, Majorca, provide a feeling of tranquillity. The wide, spreading leaves of the palms offset the hard lines of the arcade and stairs behind.*

a focus to the drawing. This can either be a farm or house set within its rural context, or, more challengingly, a large engineering structure such as a radio mast or motorway bridge. By mixing the natural and the artificial, the sketch will develop a complexity and meaning otherwise lacking if it depicts the countryside alone.

Trees can be drawn individually or as blocks. The structure of an individual tree (whether circular, columnar, pyramidal) is worth noting, but as a group the trees will form a screen like a planted wall. In urban situations trees may be planted in formal rows or grouped geometrically in a square. The challenge then is to capture their formality and to use the planted elements to complement the built ones. Often trees are employed along with shrubs and ground-cover planting. These three layers of landscape are usually designed to act together, especially in city parks. The shape of leaf, colour and texture of foliage contribute much towards the visual effect, and can be highlighted in a sketch. In more urban situations trees are mixed with paving, and here the contrast between the gnarled trunks of ancient trees and the smoother surfaces of brick or stone is deliberately exploited. Whether as an amateur artist or as a professional designer, it is worth searching out such details and learning to use them.

16.10 *Upland land-scapes (as here in this view of the Pentland Hills near Edinburgh) are usually seen from the road. Signs, poles and fences form the poorly designed fore-ground for many such views.*

16.11 *The cypress tree in this suburban street in Barcelona provides a landmark almost as important in civic terms as Antonio Gaudi's apartment block behind. The relation-ship between trees, walls, cars and build-ings establishes a bal-ance which is typical of Mediterranean towns.*

Place Dauphine, Paris
Brian Edwards '01

16.12 *The Place Dauphine in Paris provides a perfect balance between urban and landscape design. The trees have a significant impact and provide welcome shade and tranquillity within the congested city.*

16.13 *The Barcelona Pavilion, built in 1929 by Mies van der Rohe, makes little distinction between building design and landscape design. Here paving and pool are merely an extension of walls and roof.*

Interiors

Many of the rules which apply to the drawing of exterior space are equally applicable to interior volumes; in both cases one is depicting the play of solid against void, of line against plane, and light against shade. To sit and draw a room is rather like drawing a courtyard and the same general principles apply. After all, a room is little more than square with a roof, and a corridor a scaled-down street.

First, select a good place from which to view the room – a position which shows it off to best advan-

17.1 The change of level at the approach to Chapter House in Wells Cathedral enhances the ceremonial qualities of the route. The sketch exaggerates the effect by taking a low eye level. Notice how the three arches pull the eye to the top of the drawing.

tage. Choose a location which does justice to the subject, whether it be the interior of a Baroque church or of a modest café. Look at the play of light upon the surfaces, how the space is used, and how the function of the room determines its organization and level of detail. Activity, though difficult to draw, defines the function, and hence character, of the room. Some interiors are frequently empty, devoid of human bustle, whereas others are always alive with human activity. A typical pub or railway station cannot adequately be drawn or understood as a space without the rich layerings of human life found there, while the composition of the inside of a church or of a power station may benefit from their emptiness.

In sketching a scene you are seeking to understand space – the objective is to look, draw and learn. The picture is important but the heightened awareness obtained through sketching is perhaps more rewarding and ultimately more useful to the potential designer. Select your subject with care, therefore, and be critical in the approach to drawing it. If the subject is complicated, then either focus upon a detail which is typical of the whole, or abstract the view in order to pare the subject down to essentials. Never attempt too much; you will quickly tire and lose any pleasure from drawing, and the learning process will also suffer. If a complicated interior has to be recorded, then use a camera – the sketchbook is for analysis, understanding, and, one hopes, pleasure.

The sketch of the Europa Bar in Prague shows an Art Nouveau interior typical of those to be found in many European cities, from Glasgow to Moscow. The design of the space is perceived as an ellipse within a rectangle with a pair of columns defining the cross axis. In this sketch much of the detail is left out – the key elements are highlighted and Art Nouveau decoration is added to enrich the overall geometry. As the room was nearly empty at the time of the sketch, the seating level is merely hinted at, and this allows the eye to focus upon the splendid gallery and ceiling.

The Europa Bar employs a device common to turn-of-the-century interiors – it is constructed as a circle within a square treated rather like a clearing in a forest with the dome of space representing the pulling back of the trees to reveal the sky. In such an interior the columns could be likened to the trunks of trees and the exposed beams to branches. Many famous interiors employ a biological metaphor, especially those in the Art Nouveau style whose forms echo those in nature. At the Glasgow School of Art the renowned library by Charles Rennie Mackintosh has also been likened to a woodland clearing, the verticality of the columns suggesting some northern pine forest.

By way of contrast, a sketch of the interior of a medieval cathedral should evoke its imposing ambience and Gothic detail. Here the architecture is not one of line and rectilinear decoration, but of light, shade, space and carved decoration. Accordingly, the artist should adapt his or her style to suit the interior and choose materials that are appropriate for depicting the subject in question. The resulting sketch may well tell us more about Gothic architecture than could be communicated by laboriously measured drawings of walls, windows and columns, and certainly more than could a photograph.

In terms of design, interior spaces are treated in a way that is so similar to certain exterior ones that it is hardly worth analysing them as a separate en-

17.2 Church interiors are usually well-articulated spaces. Columns, arches and windows define the interior volumes and provide space for different liturgical activities. These sketches are of Wells Cathedral and deliberately focus upon the building structure.

tity. The rules of articulation, of the manipulation of scale, and of the exploitation of axial arrangements are equally relevant to the design of the interior of buildings as their exteriors. What is different is the fact that interiors are designed to be entered: these are spaces which can be inhabited and modified, rather than simply gazed upon. As such, the positioning of the artist is vital; drawings are static records yet the viewpoint should seek to show the interpenetration of space, and how light is used to illuminate a decorative panel, or to channel

17.3 *The handling of light and shade helps express the structural complexity of this fine space inside St Mark's Church in Venice. The weightiness of the columns and piers means that surface decoration is barely needed.*

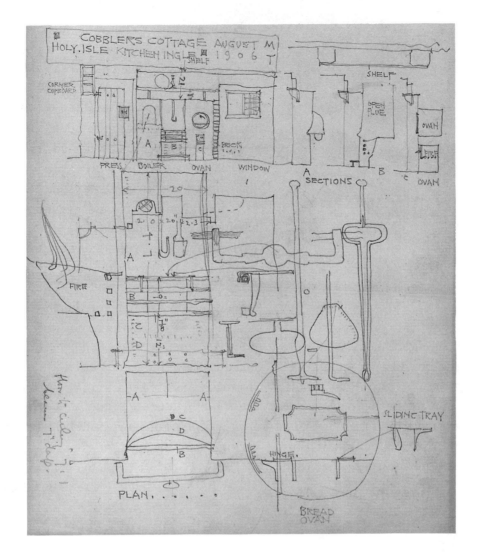

17.4 *This sketch (dated 1906) by Mackintosh of a cobbler's cottage on Holy Island superimposes plan, section and details to create a lively and informative drawing. The objective is to record every detail rather than produce a pretty drawing. Mackintosh was clearly gathering material for use later in interior design.*

17.5 *The bar of the Europa Hotel in Prague exploits a circular gallery in the centre of the room supported by Art Nouveau columns. The interior is a little like a forest clearing with light flooding down from above.*

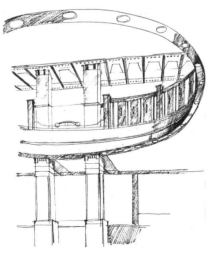
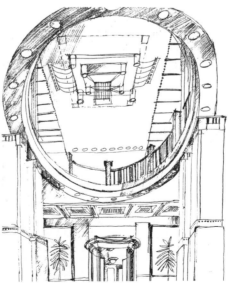
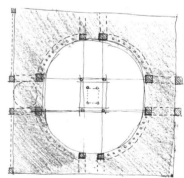

17.6 *The grotto-like quality of Parc Guell (Barcelona) by Gaudi is expressed here in a carefree drawing style. The roughly hewn stone columns and bizarre vaulting makes the space immediately memorable. Notice how the columns articulate the curved passageway.*

the visitor through rooms and corridors. Interiors, like exteriors, are experienced as linear and progressive volumes – the interplay of rooms, doorways and connecting corridors have their parallels in squares, gateways and streets. Through sketching, one may come to understand the complexity of interior design, and the essential relationships between the observer and the spaces he or she occupies.

For beginners seeking to learn how to draw and understand form, the interior as a subject offers many advantages. Sketching inside does, of course, provide shelter from the elements and generally there are fewer people peering over your shoulder than in busy city streets. In addition, interiors are normally regular spaces and hence they abide by the rules of perspective with greater clarity than do the complex angles of busy streets. Moreover, interiors are well articulated in the sense that doorways are framed by mouldings (known as architraves), walls join ceilings with a cornice, and most rooms have a focus of attention in the form of a fireplace or handsome piece of furniture. You can also move around interiors so that the sketch can become an accumulation of views or the superimposition of points of interest. Such collaging of material can make the interior sketch interesting in itself, and instructive as a piece of drawing. Hence interiors are a useful starting point for learning not only how to draw, but how to understand the rules of architectural design.

The way space is depicted tells us a great deal about how that space is used. In Le Corbusier's

17.7 *This domestic scene in Kalamazoo, Michigan, is typical of suburban life. The columns and screen wall divide the dining room from the living room without introducing unnecessary enclosure.*

17.8 *The interior of this hotel room in Barcelona opens on to the view of the street. Window shutters and the balcony provide a transition space between the interior and exterior worlds.*

17.9 *The linking of rooms is a common feature of interior design. In this apartment in Grenoble the dining room and salon are joined by double doors. The perimeter windows and the interior doors are almost on the same axis.*

sketches of the apartment-block interior at Unité, for instance, all is open, with the rooms mere zones of interconnected territory. The dividing walls barely exist, and where they do they are stripped of decoration. As a consequence, the space has little of the sense of meaning which results from applied decoration; instead, the quality of the apartment is determined by its proportions, the sense of openness, and the pictures, furniture and rugs. By way of contrast, the sketch of the 1930s ranch house in Kalamazoo, Michigan, derives its character from the decorative elements – be they columns supporting a beam or the patterned wallpaper. From such drawings we can learn that how one perceives an interior is not just to do with the relationship of shape and volume, but with the meaning given to the spaces by the applied elements of moulding, pattern and texture. Plan and section are not always adequate to explain the differences, whereas the sketch can capture the essential qualities and communicate the designer's intention or at least

the artist's interpretation of this. It is also a useful method for testing alternative ideas for improving an existing interior or for creating new designs.

The links between the inside and outside of a building are as important as those between the building and the city to which it belongs. In a building the connection between interior enclosed space and exterior open space is the doorway. This is an important perceptual element and often has symbolic value. Hence sketches of interior space are often drawn looking through a doorway, and likewise drawings of the façades of buildings frequently contain glimpses through doors or windows into the interior. The combination of these elements gives the drawings extra complexity and richness, and no little mystery.

To understand architecture is to appreciate these qualities, and the sketch is a good way to cultivate such awareness. Thus the artist should not begin a sketch in too precipitate a fashion, but only after much careful contemplation of the subject. The interior of a building reveals a more personal world, by contrast to the more public image of its exterior. Portraying the human dimension is often critical when evoking the quality of the interior – be it in the choice of furnishings, furniture or colour scheme. For instance, a room full of plants has quite a different character to one filled with paintings, or one left unembellished. Modernist interiors are often difficult to draw, but they can have a poignancy that would be lost in rooms where every surface is trimmed with mouldings and divided into panels.

The artist's choice of drawing materials and the selection of shading or colour should suit the mood or complexity of the subject. For example, unadorned modernist interiors are best rendered in washes, using pencil or magic markers to provide highlighting. Classical rooms suit pen and ink with pale-blue and pink washes. By contrast, the interiors of churches require deep tones and dark shadows to emphasize their weighty structure; yet the details need to be picked out, too, perhaps in pen or sharp pencil.

On a practical level, because the artist is unimpeded by the weather when sketching an interior, whether of a house or of a ship, train or aeroplane, he or she is free to examine it in closer detail. Hence, one's critical judgements are often sharper with regard to interiors than with any other architectural subjects. Added to this, the artist can sketch while enjoying a cup of coffee, for instance, or listening to music, and the leisurely pace engendered by mixing activities means the act of drawing becomes more enjoyable.

Since we spend most of our time in interiors we are often more aware of their shape and mood than that of city streets. Thus our drawings of interiors should be accurate with regard to both proportion and perspective. However, precisely because we are so used to occupying such spaces means that we have a tendency to sketch them in an instinctive fashion, without proper regard to the rules of perspective. If a room is regular in plan, the lines of the walls must be running to a single vanishing point even if it does not feel that that is the case. By first establishing the eye level and vanishing points, the subject will not only be easier and more rewarding to draw, but the sketch will ultimately be more valuable as a means of understanding interior space.

17.10 *The lesson to be drawn from this interior is the play of horizontal and vertical lines. The gallery and columns divide the space into units once used by the Glasgow tobacco merchants.*

17.11 *The harmonious proportions of this mosque in Mostav, Serbia, are expressed by the use of dark shading. By selecting a position on the centre line of the space, the drawing conveys something of the spiritual qualities of the interior.*

Colour

It has been recognized for some time that different areas of Britain, and indeed Europe, have their own distinctive palette of colours. Regional colour, as it is known, derives from the hues in soil and vegetation, from the colour and tone of building materials, and the effect of applied finishes such as paints. Hence southern England has a different colour range to Wales, and East Anglia to Holland across the North Sea. The dif-ferences can be explored through the sketchbook and exploited in contemporary design.

The presence of traditional regional colour is more marked in older urban areas than new, and in the countryside rather than big cities. Farming practice tends to determine the background colour in rural areas – the patchwork of greens and browns reflect both the seasons and what grows in a particular locality. Distinctive types of soil colour,

18.1 *The white-washed houses of Easdale in Argyll contrast with the dark rocks and clear blue water. Colour pencil has been employed here without secondary lines to capture the hues of this West Highland seaside village.*

133

18.2 *This scene near Guadalupe in northern Mexico mixes three elements – pencil line and shade, and colour wash – to capture the arid character of the landscape.*

18.3 *The colourful timber houses of Mendocino in northern California are recorded here in watercolour on a pen and ink base. Notice how the street scene is enlivened by gables and verandahs.*

such as that of limestone, chalk or ironstone, stain the landscape in an attractive fashion and provide the backcloth to buildings or villages. As structures are often built of local materials, they too share a range of colours not unlike those of the soil and rocks. This is particularly marked in parts of Scotland where granite-based soils and granite-built houses and bridges have a common, rather narrow, band of colours. In the south of France, red soils, parched vegetation and brick-built towns covered in sandy renders result in their own distinctive colour palette. Other areas have a tradition of applied paint finishes, such as the brightly coloured gingerbread houses of San Fransisco. Whatever the characteristics of the neighbourhood, it is surprising how regional colour varies from one area of the country to another.

To help identify ranges of regional colour it is sometimes helpful to look at the paintings of famous artists. For instance, Turner's paintings of London are quite different to those he painted of Venice – the greys, pinks and ochres of the Thames give way to golds, reds and blues when capturing the colour of the Grand Canal. Similarly, Cezanne's paintings of Provence have a different range of colours to those employed by Ceri Richards working at St Ives in Cornwall.

Urban and regional colour can usefully be explored in the freehand drawing. You can work with watercolours or coloured pencils; both are responsive to the subject, though coloured pencils or pastels are easier to use on location. You will probably find that the best representation of colour is achieved as the result of painstaking mixing and experimentation. Work to simple outlines drawn in pencil, progressing from large areas to small, and leaving out superfluous detail.

Regional colour is tending to become diluted by modern synthetic finishes. Plastic coatings on windows and cladding panels, brightly coloured advertisements and fluorescent paints have superseded much of the traditional colour palettes of our towns. The commercial forces of corporate advertising means that signs and even whole buildings compete with each other. The old colour harmonies and balance between natural and man-made elements have become a thing of the past, except in national parks and conservation areas.

18.4 Dark pencil shading focuses the eye upon the white-painted apartment house in the centre of this view in Prague. The positioning of the tree also helps frame the view and provides a point of foreground interest. The value of single trees in the city should not be over-looked.

On the other hand, there is undeniably a vibrancy and vitality of colour in modern retail parks and commercial areas of our cities. The rich colours of advertising hoardings and illuminated signs when set against the pinks and blues of solar reflecting glass can lead to very interesting sketchbook explorations. Rather than using watercolour or pencil, it is best to capture these colours in felt pen or by using opaque paints such as designers' gouache. The landscape of DIY centres is the opposite to the colour-coded historic towns that traditionalists prefer.

The study of colour may reveal particular subtleties such as the presence of colour rhythms which may be brought alive by the sketchbook. In many older streets, for instance, you will find a pattern of browns, reds, greys and whites which repeats itself in a haphazard but happy fashion. Because old buildings tend not to be particularly wide, any discordant colour is probably absorbed into the background rhythm. Added to this, applied colour in the form of painted shopfronts or windows tends to unify rather than destroy the effect.

Some places have distinctive colours which derive from the vegetation in and around their town. The use of bright flowers such as geraniums is a recurring feature of Mediterranean window sills, their colour offsetting the typical white-painted walls of that region. Likewise, cypresses give a dark-green backcloth to many seaside towns on the Adriatic coast, thereby allowing the white houses to glisten in the sunlight. A similar effect under different lighting conditions can be seen in Norwegian towns where pines provide a dark background to brightly painted timber houses. The relationship between the colour of the general vegetation, the pigments employed in painted buildings, and the coloration of rocks and soil, all combine to establish a colour code which is unique from one area of Europe to another.

The grey austerity of buildings of the post-war years has given way to the colourful façades of our post-modern age. New synthetic colours and a host of different coatings and finishes have in some areas led to what has been called 'colour pollution'. It is manifest in London Docklands where too much freedom of design has led to visual chaos. Yet some modern designers such as Michael Graves employ colour in an unashamed fashion. The 'new wave' architects seek to use colour to reinforce the organization of a building's composition – solid, dark tones at the base of their elevations, lighter browns higher up with light, sky-like colours on the roof. Hence the tripartite ordering of the masses of the building are underscored by a kind of colour narrative. By contrast, other designers seek to use colour to relate new buildings to their context – drawing upon the tones and pigments already present in the landscape and existing local buildings.

The use of colour is one of the more personal aspects of architectural design. Planning guidelines to control colour are rare, and where codes apply the results can be unsatisfactory. Left to their own devices, developers can exploit colour to commercial ends, as witnessed by most out of town shopping centres in Europe and America.

As an artist you can study local colour, analyse the source of its major ingredients, and divide the colour elements into vegetative, mineral and applied. You will find that the appearance of colours varies with the season and time of day, and this may add pleasure and complexity to your studies. The visual literacy which such investigations encourage may help you as a designer, or as a planner in formulating a colour strategy for an area.

Colour is modified by texture – that is, the surface roughness of a material. The play of light and shadow on a surface further modifies the intensity of its colour – turning heavily textured reds to brown, for instance. Outside, colour shows up the strongest when applied to a smooth surface. Hence smooth materials such as plastic or glass have greater visual impact than their colour alone would suggest. Often buildings have contrasting textures: a smoothly painted door alongside heavily textured stonework gives the wall a vibrancy which derives from the juxtapostion of different finishes and colours.

The quality of colour – of hue, luminosity and chroma – is modified by a range of environmental conditions. In addition to the varying roughness of different surfaces, one's perception of colour is equally affected by the proximity of the subject to water, the brightness of the light and the clarity of the air. In strong light shadows play an important role, often competing with the hue of a surface. Some building materials, such as corrugated sheeting, create parallel lines of shadows to complement the chroma value of the applied pigments. Similarly, materials such as paving derive their character from the competition between surface texture and colour.

The use of coloured pencils, mixed with graphite leads or watercolour and pen and ink, allows the relationship between colour and texture to be explored. Choose conditions of light which suit your subject – strong shadows for modern building materials and perhaps soft light for older, more subtle, subjects. Try to work systematically, focusing upon particular colours or the pattern in a specific locality. You may also wish to explore how the colour of materials changes in the rain or as the result of weathering over the years.

18.5 *This perpendicular church tower in Cley, Norfolk, is rendered in coloured pencil to record the tones, lines and shades of flint and stone walling, stained glass and orange pantiles.*

Chapter 19

Using drawing to analyse an urban area

CASE STUDY 1 THE MERCHANT CITY

The Merchant City area of Glasgow is typical of the kind of inner-city neighbourhood which can be analysed through drawing. By using a combination of freehand sketching and mechanical drawing it is possible to describe the main ingredients of urban form and the key role played by particular features of architecture or townscape.

Depending upon the nature of the area, the analysis could deal with the following points:
- the urban structure of the area;
- the role played by public buildings;
- the nature and characteristics of the background architecture;
- key decorative elements such as windows or doors;
- entrances and gateways;
- squares, streets, urban spaces and landscape design;
- proportional systems.

19.1 *This axonometric drawing of the Merchant City area of Glasgow shows the public buildings in black and the rest in white. Simple shade has been employed to show the approximate height of buildings relative to the width of streets. The importance of Ingram Street is highlighted by the public monuments at either end (only one survives).*

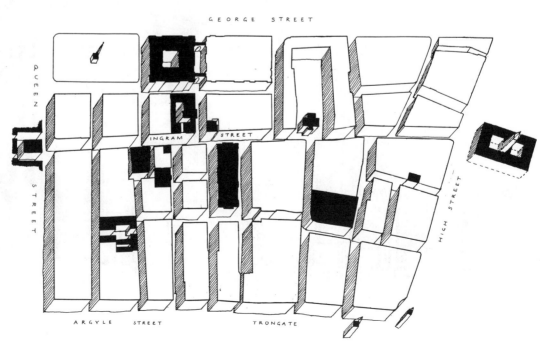

GEORGE STREET

QUEEN STREET

INGRAM STREET

HIGH STREET

ARGYLE STREET

TRONGATE

The list is not exhaustive but should seek to embrace the particular qualities that the district in question offers. As the Merchant City was a planned expansion of Glasgow in the 18th century, the layout is fairly regular and this makes the analysis a little easier than had the area grown organically. However, subsequent changes to the urban pattern and to the neighbourhood's architecture has added complexity and spatial richness, and it is largely these qualities that the freehand drawing seeks to describe and understand.

THE URBAN STRUCTURE OF THE AREA

By using a good town map, preferably an Ordnance Survey sheet, it is possible to see at a glance the basic geometry of the area. The layout of streets, the pattern of squares, the placing of public buildings are all well described on plans and can be highlighted through figure-ground analysis. Moving from the two-dimensional plan to the three-dimensional image is where drawing comes in. By employing axonometric or isometric projection, or by using bird's-eye perspective (i.e. single-point, high-level) it is possible to represent the underlying structure of the area. Such a drawing requires a degree of simplification or abstraction, otherwise the irregularities of building height or façade line would defeat all but the most gifted artists.

Drawings of urban structure do not need to show detail – their function is to represent the spatial geometry in a simple, easy-to-grasp, three-dimensional fashion. By drawing cubes of building mass which show height in proportion to width, and which relate the various urban blocks to each other, the layout of an area will become clearer than had plans alone been employed.

The method is simple: with axonometric drawing, simply rotate the plan through 45° and project the lines upwards using the same scale for building heights as the one in which the plan is drawn. With isometric drawing you will need to employ a 60°/30° setsquare and, again, do not allow for perspective in height or depth of field. Alternatively,

you can employ perspective drawing, taking a high eye-level and vanishing point placed near to the centre of the sheet. Whichever method is employed (and remember axonometric drawing is the easier to make), it helps if the sides of the blocks are shaded to highlight the three-dimensional effect.

Other key information such as the location of public buildings, parks and important squares can be added relatively easily to the basic three-dimensional drawing. The advantage of this approach to drawing is that the relationship between the urban parts becomes self-evident. For example, the importance of a public monument to a street or the role of a park in defining the edge of an area becomes a little more obvious. Had your analysis relied upon plans alone, such relationships may not have become so apparent.

THE ROLE PLAYED BY PUBLIC BUILDINGS

The three-dimensional drawing described above is also important in helping to establish the scale of influence of a public building or civic monument. A public building can have its position in the townscape eroded by unsuitable neighbours. How far the setting of a building extends can be plotted on such drawings. Often the major buildings in an area have a relationship to each other, perhaps as skyline features or as markers along a particular street. Freehand drawing can be employed to study these aspects of the townscape, particularly if such sketches are related to the drawing of the whole area. Similarly, if a design is proposed for a building, it can be tested against existing neighbours so that the potential benefits or injuries to skyline or space patterns can be analysed.

In the Merchant City public buildings are generally located so that they terminate street vistas. This classical device is common to planned towns of the 18th century. In Glasgow it means that you can find your way with ease around gridded street layouts because the ends of certain streets are differently terminated. Although the public buildings were constructed over a relatively short period,

19.2 *This isometric view shows buildings in less abstract terms than in figure 19.1. Now the public monuments are given architectural form. George Square is at the far right. The drawing distinguishes between monuments and background buildings in order to show the relationship between the two.*

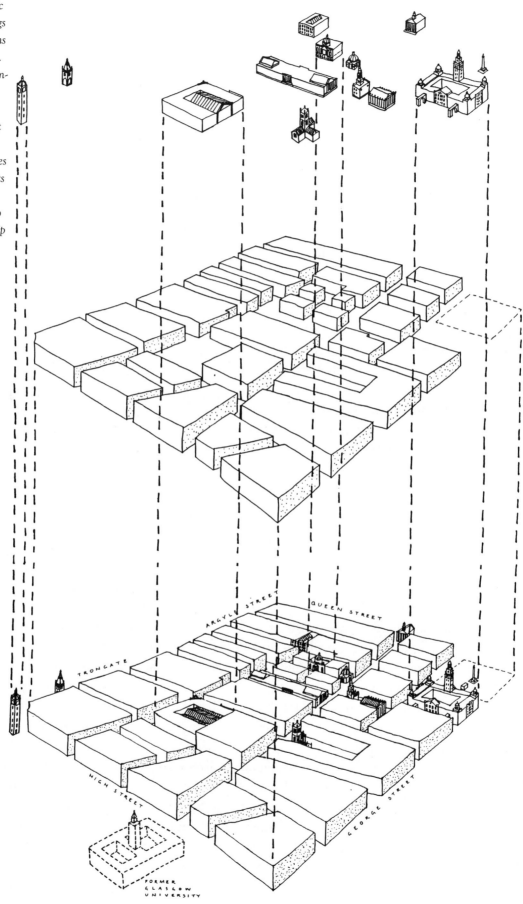

ARGYLE STREET

QUEEN STREET

TRONGATE

HIGH STREET

GEORGE STREET

FORMER GLASGOW UNIVERSITY

their styles vary from classical to Gothic, and from simple shapes to elaborate structures adorned with towers and domes. The freehand sketch allows the varying ambitions of the different architects to be recorded and analysed. You will find that certain roads like Ingram Street are terminated at one end, in this case by the former Royal Exchange (now the Stirling Library) which has a handsome portico projecting into the street space. The other end of this straight street opens on to the derelict east end of Glasgow. Thus a sketch of the street could not only highlight its distinctive qualities, but could form the basis for speculative proposals for terminating the open end.

Public buildings have a scale and presence greater than that of the background architecture. Although in the Merchant City they are not necessarily taller than their neighbours (except the City Chambers), they employ columns, pediments and domes to establish their position in the architectural hierarchy. The use of decoration and visual codes can be the subject of a drawing, especially if it is related to the pedestrian's experience of the city.

In the Merchant City many public buildings have changed their function since they were built. Mention has been made of the former Royal Exchange now being used as a public libary, but there are also churches which currently serve as night clubs, restaurants or theatres, and market buildings which are concert halls. The ability of monuments to adapt to new public uses is an argument of Aldo Rossi's in his *Architecture of the City*, and is well represented in Glasgow. The important point is to realize that the visual currency of places like the Merchant City depends upon the survival of the inherited public buildings.

THE NATURE AND CHARACTERISTICS OF THE BACKGROUND ARCHITECTURE

The background architecture of the Merchant City determines the physical context for the public buildings. Whether the everyday buildings are houses, offices or warehouses, they are the back-

19.3 *The termination of Ingram Street by the Stirling Library (formerly the Royal Exchange) makes a dramatic sketch. The drawing is rendered with sunlight on the main façade and shadows expressing the depth of the colonnade. Notice how the eye is taken into the adjoining spaces by the arcade to the right.*

cloth to urban life and contribute significantly to the character of this inner-city area. The relationship between the function of an area, its buildings and how they are decorated are worthy subjects for sketchbook exploration.

The character of residential neighbourhoods in the Merchant City depends upon whether apartment blocks, tenements or converted warehouses are the main type of housing. Each has a different relationship to the street and a different form of exterior expression. Likewise, the degree to which housing is mixed with shops or work spaces determines not just the appearance but use of exterior space.

The industrial areas, too, have their own character. The presence of cranes, bollards, heavy doors and robust materials give the workshop and industrial areas qualities which are immediately recognizable. Even the modern factory buildings such as the *Glasgow Herald* printing works incorporate similar industrial features.

The main business district is also distinctive; the perpendicular façades of modern office blocks and their sheer glass walls create unique townscapes. They are a challenge to the artist since decorative elements are normally in short supply; one has to rely upon plane, surface texture and parallel line. When an historic church or old house is marooned in such areas, a rendition of the relative scale and degree of decoration can lead to a telling drawing.

KEY DECORATIVE ELEMENTS SUCH AS WINDOWS OR DOORS

The design and detailing of windows and doors help establish the style of architecture. The use of decorative surrounds picked out in stone, brick or timber allow us to categorize buildings into particular styles, and often provide clues to their date of construction. Also the use of specific technologies in the design and fabrication of windows and doors tells us a great deal about the technology of the age that produced them. For example, the narrow width of Georgian windows and their subdivision into many small panes of glass provide insights into the structural limitations of the age and the specific problems experienced by the glaziers of 18th-century Glasgow in the production of glass. Similarly, the design and detailing of Georgian doorways give clues to the symbolic value of building entrances, and to the level of sophistication achieved by joiners at the time. Added to this, the proportional elegance of such doors suggest that even in provincial towns the language of the pattern book had been well assimilated.

Whole buildings are complex and frequently daunting subjects to draw and you may instead prefer to concentrate your attention upon doors or windows. The architect often invests a great deal of time in the design of these elements, which makes them particularly worthy subjects for free-hand sketches. As doors and windows are openings into a building, they are frequently framed in a distinctive fashion, and sometimes given symbolic value by the addition of figurative sculpture or lettering. Windows are normally dark openings crisscrossed by glazing bars in an attractive design. With the addition of blinds, curtains and shutters, the window provides a good subject for the artist, with its layers of different materials not normally depicted in architectural drawing. Although windows allow light into buildings, they also permit those on the inside to look out. Hence the world of the interior and exterior have their interface at the window, making another worthy subject for a sketch.

19.4 This sketch of Hutcheson Street being terminated by Hutcheson's Hospital (Glasgow home of the National Trust for Scotland) exploits the verticality of the streets in the Merchant City. Although the original street pattern survives, this view shows how much the architecture has changed over the years. Note how the perpendicular lines of the buildings arrest the movement of the eye down the street.

19.5 As the termination of streets by public buildings is such a feature of the area, any graphic analysis should focus upon this theme. Here Robert Adam's Trades House (1794) acts as a focal point to Garth Street. It is framed by buildings whose height is the same as the width of the street.

19.6 Carved stone detailing such as this city coat of arms high on a church gable is typical of the older buildings.

19.7 *This view of George Square shows the dominating presence of the City Chambers (Town Hall), built in 1880. The vanishing point is along George Street on the left. Notice how statuary provides a focus to the square, which in this drawing excludes the trees and people.*

In the Merchant City doors and windows come in many forms. In the warehouse areas many are plain and with repetitive forms, yet they establish interesting rhythms or patterns in the street scene. The subdivision of larger windows into smaller openings and the grouping together of these into tall bands give such areas their distinctive character. In some of the new apartment buildings circular windows have been used to express major street corners or to give verve to the design of rooftops.

When drawing windows and doors, it is often useful to exploit shadows. The set-back of windows within their frames allows a shadow line to be established which then becomes a major element in the composition of the sketch. The depth of shadow should reflect the distance the window or door is set back within its frame, although when drawing this some licence is permitted. Each pane of glass or timber panel would also have a shadow, which provides a secondary layer of articulation. If the door or window is framed in columns with a pediment, these bigger architectural elements form a bold frame which imposes an order on the drawing – an order which makes visual reference, perhaps, to the larger structure of the building's façade. The various components of the subject will have their own scale, pattern and proportion – and it is these elements which should attract the architectural draughtsman's attention.

Modern doorways can be quite minimal in design, but the need for handles and hinges, and even security cameras, makes them interesting subjects. Like traditional doorways, the change of level at the threshold and the presence of signage and perhaps interior planting, can provide material for a telling sketch.

To assess your local environment graphically, you should look at the details as well as the whole. The quality known as townscape is to be found in both the whole urban scene and in many of its smaller parts, such as windows and doors. Often the details are changed unsympathetically whereby the broader view, though structurally much the same, is gradually devalued.

ENTRANCES AND GATEWAYS

Every neighbourhood or district has its boundaries and hence entrance buildings. As we saw in Chapter 13, these may not be self-evident; sometimes you have to search them out, or to see such structures as hotels or pubs as gateway buildings. Just as every neighbourhood has its centre and a few special, often public, buildings, so too you will probably have a perception of the edges to the area and its entrances. In the Merchant City such entrance buildings may be recognized, for instance, in the cliffs of sandstone tenements and wide straight streets penetrating into the heart of the area and flanked by gateway shops (such as Marks & Spencer's in Glassford Street).

The personal nature of a sketch will result in different people viewing the same place in different ways. Consequently, your perception of the entrances and gateways in an urban district – and this applies equally to the Merchant City – will differ from someone else's. But this is the strength of the sketch: unlike the camera, which can only record the same view no matter who pushes the shutter, a drawing is able to express different meanings and interpretations of a scene.

SQUARES, STREETS, URBAN SPACES AND LANDSCAPE

The gridiron layout of the Merchant City gives the streets a particular distinction. Planned in the 18th century, the area is not unlike parts of Chicago or New York – straight streets with right-angled junctions leading into leafy squares. Indeed, the streets are more important than many of the buildings, which merely provide the backcloth to urban life. The framing of the streets, their periodic punctuation by key buildings, and the fashion in which streets are linked to squares or churchyards, makes them a subject worthy of sketchbook analysis.

To obtain such drawings means, of course, that you have to work within the space of the street. The bustle, fumes and noise do not make for comfortable freehand drawing, and such aids as rulers are essential if speed is important. If you are concentrating upon street space, then the activities of the street may be important. The relationship between the function of the buildings that line the street and how, as at the Italian Centre in John Street, the public space is modified by it may be central to the quality of place and therefore to its portrayal in your sketch.

It is useful to get to know an area before starting to draw; note-taking can help to save frustration later on. What you will need to jot down are the best times to draw with regard to the angle of light and levels of activity, the position of terminating buildings (to provide visual stops to the gridiron layout) and places where greenery can soften the harsh lines of the drawing. If your sketch focuses exclusively upon the perpendicular lines of modern office buildings, then noting the best times for lighting effects could prove useful, as well as recording how such buildings relate to the street.

Tone, line and texture are useful techniques to exploit in such drawings. The rectilinear nature of modern streets and the canyon-like edges formed by modern buildings are best rendered in conté, crayon, pen or soft pencil. Where a particular building or tree stands in contrast to the remainder of the scene, it can be drawn in a different material, thereby adding complexity to the sketch.

PROPORTIONAL SYSTEMS

Many of our urban environments have evolved under the influence of building codes or planning regulations. Much of the New Town of Edinburgh grew up under a rule limiting buildings to three storeys, and the same was true of the Bloomsbury area of London. In many Victorian cities the buildings could not be higher than the width of the streets they faced because of the restrictions placed on them by the Municipal Building Acts. The effect was to lead to a certain monotony of layout, particularly in working-class districts where 'mean houses faced mean streets'.

In spatial terms, however, the regulations often led to a rather classical sense of order. Where the

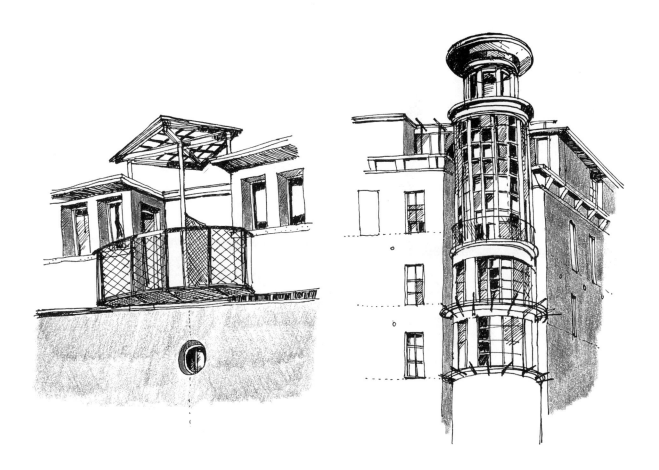

19.8 New buildings bring with them modern details. These windows can be found in recent apartment blocks constructed in the area.

19.9 *The silhouette of the Merchant City is as distinctive as its ground plan. Here the City Chambers and the tower of Hutcheson's Hospital are shown as viewed from the author's apartment in Ingram Square.*

buildings were high and the streets wide, a generous cube of space existed in the front of each building. The harmonious relationship between buildings and space engendered by such regulations were often reflected in the subdivision of the façades of buildings. In many 19th-century towns, and particularly in the Merchant City, a proportional system can be traced in both urban layout and building design.

Recent development in Glasgow has departed from the earlier pattern, and now modern buildings are higher relative to the street width than were their predecessors. The same is true of Edinburgh, London and even Boston, which grew up under similar influences.

Sketching proportional systems requires detailed analysis. You will need to look at the relationship of the various parts (buildings to streets, windows to walls, streets to squares) and record them through plan, section and elevation as well as the freehand sketch. An understanding of the inherited geometry of places is particularly useful if, as a student of architecture or a designer, you intend to make speculative proposals for the redevelopment of a site, or, as a member of the public, you wish to object to the overdevelopment of a particular site.

A grasp of proportion is also important when drawing a complicated building so that its different sections are represented accurately. Buildings which are full of ornate detail or complex structural systems are not easy for the beginner to draw. By dividing the building into parts, each based upon an expressed structural system such as columns or a repeating pattern of windows or storey heights, a complex building can be reduced to its constituent parts. Once the basic subdivisions are in place and each has at least an approximation to reality, then the detail can be added later.

The advantage of breaking down a complex subject into simple subdivisions is to draw attention to the proportional systems behind the design. Often the proportions of a fine building are disguised by over-elaborate decoration or an array of recent signs. If as an artist you can see beyond the surface embellishment, you may uncover a proportional code which not only helps you draw the building, but provides clues to design guides which could be adopted in the future, should you have ambitions towards being a planning officer, architect or developer.

146

CASE STUDY 2 THE BASTIDE TOWNS, FRANCE

The Bastide towns in the Dordogne region of France represent a unique collection of small country towns eminently suitable for a sketchbook study. Built as new, fortified settlements in the 13th century by different sovereigns, including the English king Edward I, each town contains a central market square surrounded by handsome arcades. A common range of elements is found in each of the dozen or so towns; besides an arcaded market square there is generally a timber-framed market hall, a centrally placed church used originally for defensive purposes, a town wall with gateways, and a gridded layout of streets. These elements make for a remarkable consistency in spite of the different origins of the towns. For whilst Edward I laid out Beaumont and Lalinde, Villeréal, Castillonnes and Eymet were new towns founded by the local monarch Alfonse de Poitiers.

The Bastide towns are grouped in a fertile region about 25 miles square, west and south of Bergerac in south-west France. Each occupies, or overlooks, a valley bottom since the agricultural development of the surrounding marshes was the principal starting point for the towns. As their economy grew, so too did their architecture. Houses, often restricted to three storeys high, blossomed with first Gothic, then Renaissance decoration, reflecting the wealth of the merchants and farmers who flourished under aristocratic protection. Civic buildings quickly became more imposing, leaving a splendid heritage today. As the latter are grouped around or stand within the market square, their impact is both immediate and impressive.

Since the Bastide towns were developed according to a predetermined plan, they have a clarity that is unusual in medieval settlements. The square street blocks, central market place and clearly defined town edges (usually formed by a defensive wall or river) result in places which are well ordered and legible in architectural terms. In most cases the centre of the town is marked by a church or market hall, the main commercial activities are grouped within the arcade around the central square, and the secondary streets support private houses and small shops. With gated entrances or approaches via medieval river bridges, the sequence from outside to inside is also well articulated.

The unusual qualities of urban design represented by the Bastide towns make them a fine subject for sketchbook exploration. As cafés and bars are grouped around the market square, drawings of the square and its contents can be prepared in some comfort from well-located positions.

19.10 *These town plans drawn from tourist maps help to explain the structure of the central squares of two of the Bastide towns of the Dordoyne – Eymet (a) and Villeréal (b).*

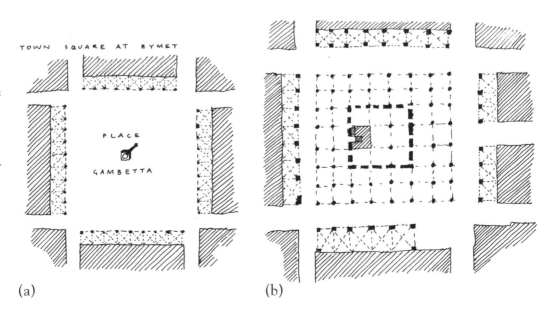

(a)   (b)

Several drawings are required to gain a full understanding of even fairly modest towns. In the case of the Bastide towns, a series of sketches can perhaps capture the sequence of views from the town edge to the centre, focusing upon key elements such as the gateways, arcades and public buildings.

Since the Bastide towns have characteristic layouts, picture postcards often show them from the air. These views can be adapted by the artist to show the structure of each particular town, thereby supplementing the street sketches with more analytical drawings. Detailed maps also show the town layout and these allow the geometry of street blocks, position of arades and market halls to be plotted. Combining sketches, axonometric views and figure-ground plans can result in an informed exploration of the subject.

Having studied the urban structure of the Bastide towns, the next step is to record the design of specific buildings. You might choose to focus on market halls, for example, where expressive carpentry could be the attraction; or upon private houses, which vary from modest structures to those

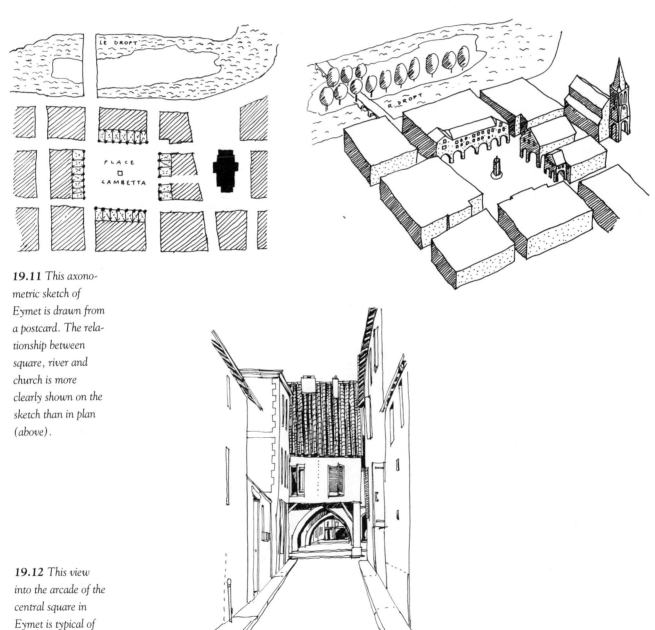

19.11 *This axonometric sketch of Eymet is drawn from a postcard. The relationship between square, river and church is more clearly shown on the sketch than in plan (above).*

19.12 *This view into the arcade of the central square in Eymet is typical of the Bastide towns.*

19.13 *The market hall in Villeréal fills the central space. This sequence of sketches explores the progression from outside the square to the area beneath the timber floor of the market hall.*

with sculpted doorways, ornate window surrounds and splendid street-fronting courtyards. Hence in a few days the character of the Bastide towns can be studied and sketched, from the whole town to the details of individual buildings.

Rather than drawing subjects at random, the selection of particular themes gives a sense of purpose to the task of sketching that is both enjoyable and educational for the artist. In addition, the advantage of sketching small towns is their relative simplicity of design and lack of bustle. The modest Bastide towns demonstrate the advantages of a pre-determined town plan which contains well-defined edges and a clear civic focus in the centre. The lay-out of such towns offers lessons, perhaps, for our age with its ribbon development, poorly maintained central areas and lack of skyline definition. Like nearly all plantation towns, the new settlements of the Bastides brought with them a sense of geometric unity. It is this spatial and civic order which the sketchbook can record, and which is sadly lacking from the current proposals for urban villages.

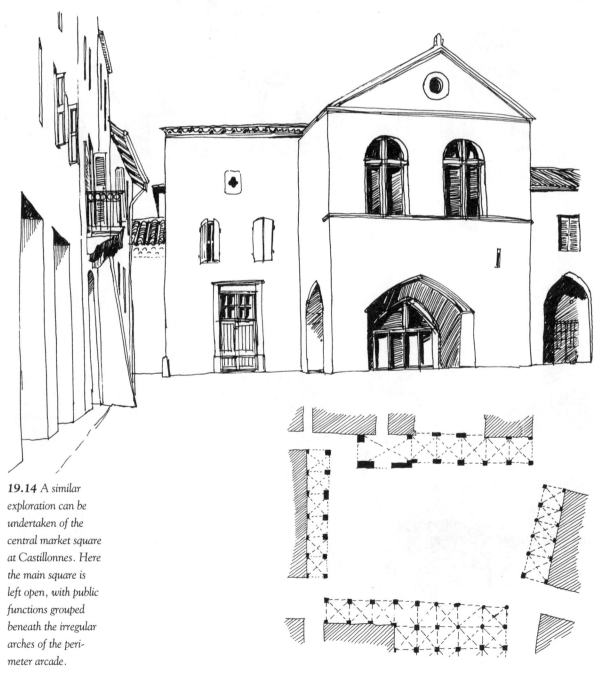

19.14 *A similar exploration can be undertaken of the central market square at Castillonnes. Here the main square is left open, with public functions grouped beneath the irregular arches of the perimeter arcade.*

Part Four
The Way Forward

Chapter 20

Exploration through the sketch-book – some suitable subjects

Developing a personal appreciation of buildings and places through the sketchbook benefits from a structured approach. The pursuit of design experience via the freehand drawing requires an allocation of time and the selection of topics relevant to your urban inquiries. Rather than try to draw a whole town, it is often useful to focus upon part of a neighbourhood or a particular topic and explore it systematically. For example, you may decide to concentrate upon one street and show how its character changes from one end to another. Alternatively, you could focus your attention on a square or courtyard, recording how the buildings relate to the space, and how people interact with it.

As a student exercise it is often valuable to record and analyse through the sketchbook the key qualities of places, from their skyline to the spaces between buildings and the edges of districts. In fact a systematic exploration of topics along the following lines can heighten one's personal understanding of places.

KEY STREETS

Choose a street with which you are familiar and sketch interesting buildings or details such as distinctive façades, signs or shopfronts, or spaces set back from the street. Once you have walked along the street a few times, storing in your mind the key qualities and significant buildings, your next task is to record them through the freehand sketch and perhaps to locate them on a sketch plan of the street. Some points to note might be the positions and design of signs, changes in the angle of the street, and deliberate points of punctuation. If the street is a major one, you will probably find important shops or civic buildings located along it.

Once the exploration is complete and you have a collection of sketches and a plan, you can then begin to analyse the street by noting the critical factors in its design. Although valuable in itself and in your growing awareness of places, the exercise could lead to you suggesting changes in the design of the street to enhance its qualities. Sites for new buildings could be identified and sketch designs prepared, or suggestions could be made for tree planting or even traffic management.

Part of your exploration could involve the study of façades of buildings along the street. The patterns of windows, the rhythm created by the varying widths and heights of buildings and the different materials employed in their construction make good subjects for sketchbook analysis. Your drawings may consist of both a formal study of the street, in which detail is edited out, or a descriptive rendering which captures such features as texture and colour.

URBAN SPACES

Select a space in your town and record through the freehand drawing its key features. These may include public buildings such as libraries or the town hall, or – if the space is a residential square – perhaps repeating house fronts. The degree to which the space is enclosed, the height of the surrounding buildings, and any features such as sculpture or trees in the centre of the square, should all attract the artist's attention.

If the square is large and complex, then you will probably have to focus your attention on a single aspect of it. If, say, you decide to explore how the library relates to the square, then you could draw the façade of the library, its entrance, and the way the doors open out from the space. Many public buildings have a gathering space outside the entrance, perhaps sheltered beneath a columned portico. Often major squares are landmarked by a tower or spire and this, too, could form the subject of your personal exploration.

In smaller residential squares, the use of shared balconies, communal drying areas or playgrounds for children may be an important feature. Such courtyards are frequently jam-packed with cars or filled with dense greenery, and again this could provide a fruitful topic for sketching.

SKYLINE

The study of skyline and silhouette shows how important tall buildings are to the character of different towns. Many cities are marked by distinctive skylines: London's Houses of Parliament (and particularly Big Ben), the Eiffel Tower in Paris, the Empire State Building in New York, all give a unique stamp to the urban silhouette. Lesser towns have their own characteristic skylines, too, though on a smaller scale. Places like Guildford, with its 20th-century cathedral, and Motherwell, with its collection of chimneys and cooling towers associated with the nearby steelworks, have skylines which

20.1 *The sketch of Penicuik high street in Scotland shows the rhythm of house fronts. The sketch records the curve of the street and shows how the house in the distance becomes a focus and deflects the eye around the bend.*

155

20.2 *This pair of sketches of the coal-mining town of Newtongrange in Midlothian shows the relationship of the terraced houses to small public squares. The urban spaces (these days often poorly maintained) were to provide sunlight, recreation and a measure of amenity for these impoverished communities.*

shape the perception people hold of the towns.

Drawing skylines requires a bold approach and much use of dark shading. The skyline should ideally be drawn from both inside and outside the town, and from different angles. You may well find that tall structures denote the town centre, acting as markers to the commercial core. It may be, however, that the tallest buildings are the least interesting. Many modern office and apartment blocks are dreary structures, while the lower church spires are more profiled and hence worthier of note.

When sketching the skyline, one is also free to use one's imagination to modify the silhouette of the town. By re-profiling tower blocks or by adding new structures to the roof, the shape of the building can be changed to the benefit of the city skyline. As most of the high buildings in Britain were built in the 1960s and 1970s when the aspirations of building design were not very high, the opportunity exists to use the sketches to speculate upon how such structures could be enriched to improve the skyline and hence legibility of our towns.

NEIGHBOURHOODS

Big towns are really a collection of villages of which each is a separate entity, a neighbourhood shaped by distinctive building types (terraced houses, semi-detached, tenements, flats) or different land uses (offices, warehouses, educational areas). Land use is usually reflected in building type, reinforcing the sense that a big town is really a collection of different neighbourhoods each with its own characteristic architecture.

Freehand drawing is a good tool to use in analysing neighbourhoods. First choose an area that is not too large or too complex to draw. Determine the boundaries of the area, its centre and key urban and architectural qualities. Study where the public spaces are and how they are designed. Look at how different neighbourhoods are defined by major traffic routes or natural features such as hills or rivers.

Sketch the major building types in order to record and understand their form. Look at how

buildings and spaces are arranged in plan form and perhaps in section. Draw characteristic details such as bay windows and entrance porches if you are dealing with a residential area, or glazing grids and office doorways if you are sketching a commercial neighbourhood.

The heightened awareness achieved by such an exploration allows students of architecture and design to intervene in a fashion which enhances, rather than destroys, the inherited patterns. The task of the urban designer should be to strengthen the character and culture of places and to add new richness. Places should be visually firm and well structured, with additions reinforcing the existing style of the neighbourhood.

BOUNDARIES AND BARRIERS

Towns, and even the countryside, consist of places with marked boundaries. These are often natural features such as rivers, but they can be railway lines, motorways and embankments. These barriers help divide the city and its surrounding countryside into parcels with clearly defined edges. Edges, corridors and boundaries are rewarding subjects to draw because of the way buildings interact with them. In London, for instance, the Thames forms a major barrier between the two halves of the conurbation. The river itself is lined with warehouses, office and apartment blocks, and the occasional public building. The bridges create links between the two edges, giving them a particular significance. If you take a river bus in London or Paris, you quickly become aware of the qualities the river has as a corridor with firm urban edges.

Similarly, to drive along urban motorways is to be aware of the edges formed by these vast concrete structures which divide the city into huge parcels of land. A study of how buildings interact with these barriers is important to both the architect and town planner.

Roads often define the limits of our cities: a ring road, for instance, may constitute an urban boundary – built up on the city side and left green on the other. In sketching boundaries the task of the artist

FRAMES ENTRANCE INTO CIRCUS

Down hill

WIDENING OF ROAD

Into Circus

ONE HOUSE WIDTH.

view framed by plane tree

over my stepping down slope. -pattern, rhythm of stone colours

Train over city

Detain

20.3 *The streets of Bath provide an opportunity to study urban proportions. These quick sketches mix details with general views and employ simple graphics to augment freehand drawing.*

20.4 *This busy small square in central Barcelona benefits from the presence of a mature tree. The curving line of the street provides a fine sweep of building façades at the corner of the square.*

20.5 *Fragments of buildings can be rewarding, especially if as well articulated as this Glasgow apartment block.*

BUILDING TYPES

Most towns consist of a collection of distinctive building types whose qualities and variety are representative of the area. The three-bedroomed semi-detached villa is typical of southern England, the terraced house of the Midlands, and the tenement of Scotland. By selecting a specific building type you can explore its various manifestations within a neighbourhood or geographical area, relating the elevation of different buildings to aspects of their plan. Such an exploration through the freehand sketch can highlight regional differences and teach you about the traditions of your area.

Your exploration could embrace factory buildings, offices, warehouses and churches as well as residential buildings. By selecting a specific building type and studying the permutations of form and arrangement in a precise area, it is surprising how many examples can be discovered and their variety of design. In addition, focusing upon selected building types encourages you to become knowledgeable about the design of that particular category of buildings. In the past, schools of architecture required their students to keep a sketchbook of buildings, categorizing arrangements of plan and elevation within specific building types. Besides cultivating an appreciation of the links between the design of the building plan and the treatment of the façade, the use of sketchbooks also encouraged the students to learn from past examples rather than seeking to design new building types from scratch.

BUILDING DETAILS

If whole buildings or engineering structures are too complex for your needs or drawing skills, then select an aspect of their architecture or construction. You could concentrate on a relatively simple subject such as windows, chimneys or roofs, or alternatively you could attempt the more difficult topic of shopfronts, curtain walling or decorative paving. Whatever subject is selected, ensure you locate the example clearly and use a drawing style

is to search out examples of continuity and discontinuity. Edges are best when they are visually firm and well defined. One could perhaps explore a river or motorway, noting and sketching strong and weak points. Rivers often flow through fragmented areas, such as older docklands, passing through to well-regulated townscapes in the city centre. By selecting particular viewpoints you can explore these physical barriers, noting in the process areas where the edges should be better defined, or where the barrier may be bridged by some form of new structure.

20.6 The imposing suburb of Pollokshields in Glasgow provides ample material for the sketchbook. Here houses with bay windows and turrets look on to leafy gardens.

which allows one example to be compared with another. It is remarkable how much pleasure you will derive from building up a collection of examples drawn from your neighbourhood or on your travels. You will be surprised, too, at how freshly you view your local environment once you have taken the time to record and analyse it through the freehand sketch.

EXPLORING YOUR LOCAL HERITAGE

Sketching is an excellent way to study your local architectural or archaeological heritage. You do not have to be a great artist to benefit from the heightened awareness of the subject which drawing it gives. The exploration of one's locality through the freehand sketch can be supplemented by accurately measured surveys or searches through documentary sources. No matter where one lives, the local environment will provide much material for those intent upon exploring a town's heritage.

Whether you choose to study the conservation of town houses, rural farms or industrial monu-

ments, drawing on location is an essential starting point. Such studies can deal with building types which may interest you – perhaps the arrangement of farm buildings outside your town – or with special parts of the town such as conservation areas. If you are drawing primarily for pleasure, then seek out attractive compositions and comfortable locations, but if your sketch is part of more systematic analysis, then you should adopt a more methodical approach.

For example, if you are studying farm buildings, start with a specific building type, such as threshing barns, or particular farm layouts, whether U-shaped or based around a courtyard. The important point is to build up a collection of sketched case studies which can be compared in both general form and detail. In no time you will be surprised at the similarities which exist between subjects and the subtle evolutions of form that emerge in response to changing farm practices or different climatic demands. By analysing a specific building type fairly closely, your knowledge of the local environment and its architectural heritage may

20.7 *This street of urban tenements in Glasgow exploits the compositional possibilities of bay windows. The terrace forms a crescent around a shallow planted square.*

20.8 *Many inner-city areas contain the houses of once prosperous merchants. These two villas are from a 19th-century district of Vancouver. Notice how both houses exploit the outer edge of the building by providing verandahs, bay windows and raised walkways.*

well exceed the documentation available in local libraries. It may be possible to compare your field sketches and notes with historic maps of the area, allowing you to speculate upon the development of particular farm types in your neighbourhood. Such exercises have obvious value in environmental education and could be used to support the conservation of such buildings if they are threatened by planning applications.

If you are seeking to analyse historic buildings in your neighbourhood through the medium of freehand drawing, you may find it useful to add sketch plans or details of such things as windows or gate hinges to the space around the edges of your drawing. A single sheet can then provide a wide range of useful documentary material. This supplementary material may prove useful if you are seeking to date the building or identify the people who built it.

EXPLORING DESIGN: THE WORK OF FOUR GREAT ARCHITECTS

There is a great deal which can be learnt from the careful study of the buildings by famous architects. How they fashion a corner, model a façade, or organize the ground plan are useful fields of inquiry. Armed with a sketchbook and plenty of time, the student should be able to visit a building and through descriptive or analytical drawings come away with an enhanced appreciation of architectural design.

It is remarkable how many buildings by famous architects exist in most European cities. Wherever you live, it should be possible to analyse a building of real worth. As a resident of Glasgow, I have the works of Charles Rennie Mackintosh and Alexander 'Greek' Thomson on my doorstep, and should I live in Edinburgh or London, I would have the buildings of Robert Adam or Richard Rogers to explore. The examples given here are from Glasgow's two great architects, together with sketchbook studies of Le Corbusier's Ronchamp Chapel and various buildings by Antonio Gaudi. Sketches of works by the latter are the result of visits to France and Spain specifically to experience, record and explore the works of these two fine European architects.

It is important to seek out the works of major architects. Experiencing buildings and places first hand is infinitely more valuable than studying their designs by way of slides and construction

20.9 *The Norman carving on the capital of each of the nave columns at Bayeux Cathedral varies from one column to the next. This sketch is one of a series that chart the differences along the nave.*

drawings. The sketch heightens the act of experience, and forces the observer into a critical relationship with the subject. A systematic approach is desired, though many undertake the freehand drawing in a more spontaneous fashion.

Depending upon the building, the sketchbook analysis will probably move from the exploration of the whole to the detail, and from the edge to the interior. Such features as entranceways and staircases might deserve a specific sketch, as would windows or railing details in the case of an architect such as Mackintosh. The general sketch may relate the structure to its context, showing perhaps how the building interacts with the pavement that edges it. The analysis may include a sketch plan or section to show how the external form relates to the plan of the building. Drawings help unravel the complex parameters under which designers operate, making clear their architectural intentions.

By examining the work of different architects, the student of design gains insights into the diverse philosophies in operation. It is evident in the illustrations included here that while Mackintosh is concerned with abstract forms and shapes, Thomson is stretching the classical language almost to breaking point. While Le Corbusier employs heavy concrete walls to create a monu-

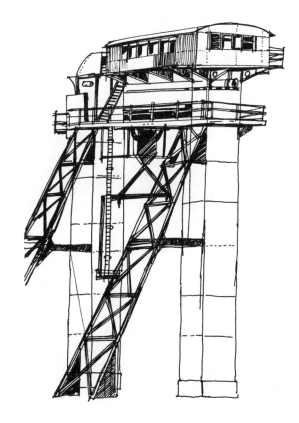

20.10 *Industrial architecture provides some of the most sculptural subjects for those intent on learning about design. This crane is to be found at Harwich.*

20.11 *These drawings of buildings by Mackintosh seek to explore how he handles design. His bold massing and contrast beween horizontal and vertical lines, and between solid and void, are the basis for these studies.*

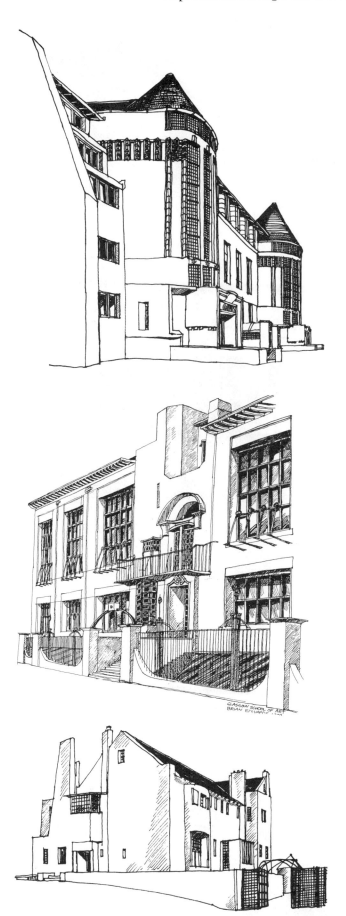

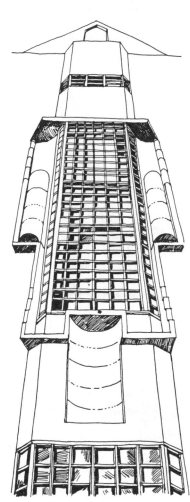

20.12 *Alexander Thomson is recognized as a master of street architecture. This graphic study of his buildings in Glasgow focuses upon his handling of façades.*

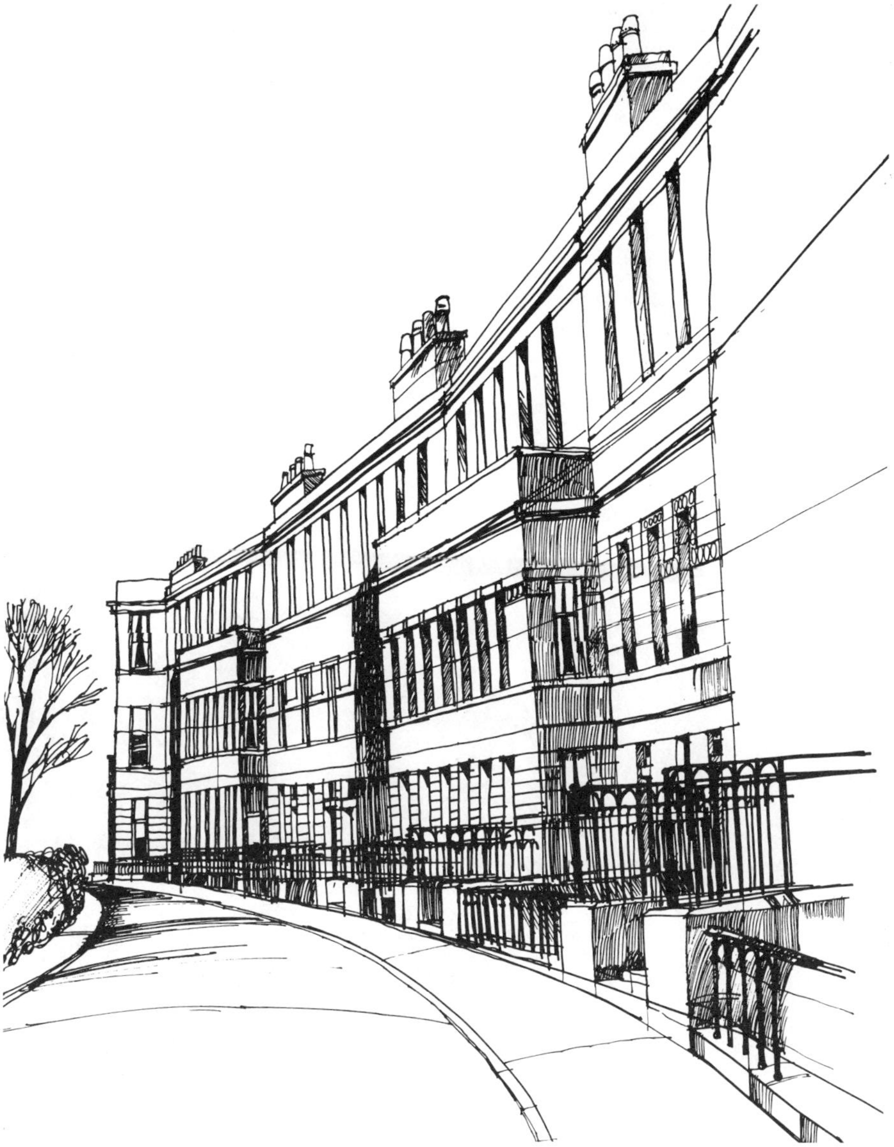

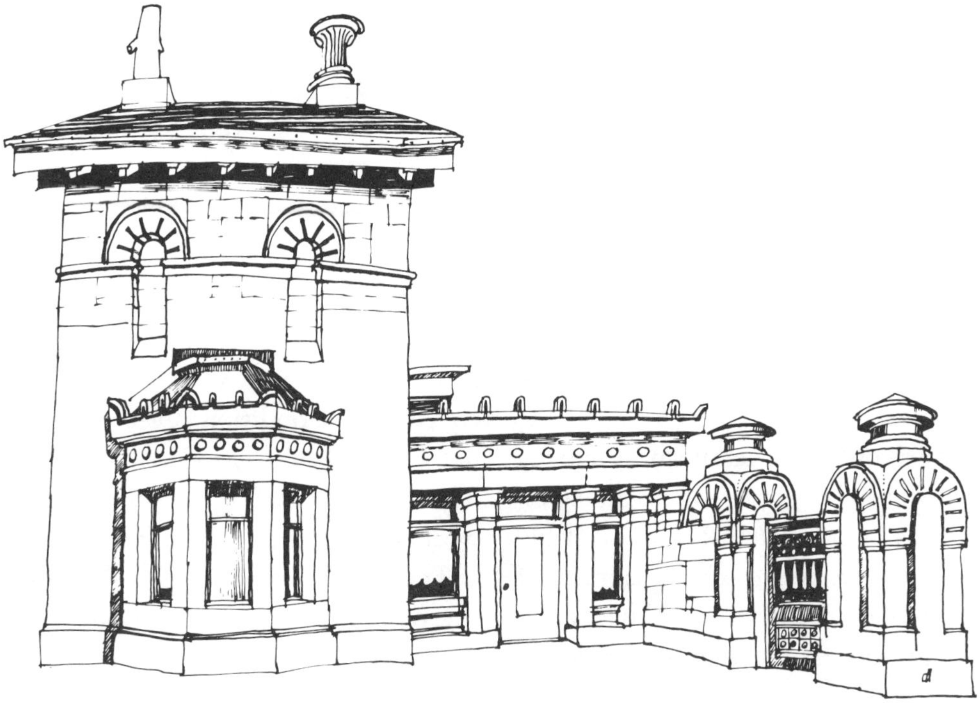

20.13 *Antonio Gaudi built several notable apartment blocks in Barcelona at the turn of the century. How he composed the façade around flowing lines is of interest here.*

mental modernity, Gaudi breaks the surface into decorative flowing lines derivative of natural or organic shapes.

By focusing upon a specific issue of design, the sketch should be selective in spirit. It is of little value to strive to record every detail whilst missing the fundamental truth. No matter where one lives, there are examples of good architecture available to help teach lessons in design. Our accumulated wisdom as designers resides in the buildings round about us. Both the successes and failures of design

are to be found in most towns, even those lacking the works of well-known architects. Armed with an appetite for sketching, the student should gain useful insights into what has been built, thereby continuing a tradition. Of course, good design is not a case of blindly repeating the language of the inherited monuments, but of inventing new forms by changing the angle of refraction.

The sketch teaches how to look and learn from the past without inhibiting movement into the future.

20.14 *Le Corbusier's chapel at Ronchamp has lessons for those interested in church architecture. His handling of shape, light and space is the main interest of his sketches.*

Chapter 21

From sketch to design

Having become accustomed to using the sketchbook as an aid to visual understanding, it is not too much of a leap to begin thinking in design terms. Your sketches will not only have sharpened your perceptual awareness, but more importantly opened your eyes to how a designer thinks. Basically an architect or urban designer has to evolve a form – hopefully an elegant one – to suit a particular function, and relate it to a context. Hence design is a two-way process

– working from the functional programme outwards, and from the physical surroundings inwards. How well the balance is struck establishes the appropriateness and even beauty of the design.

Most books on design focus upon programme, process and function, leaving aside questions of suitability to townscape or landscape. By way of contrast, this book looks at the visual language of places in an attempt to address the balance. Drawing existing buildings, squares and streets not

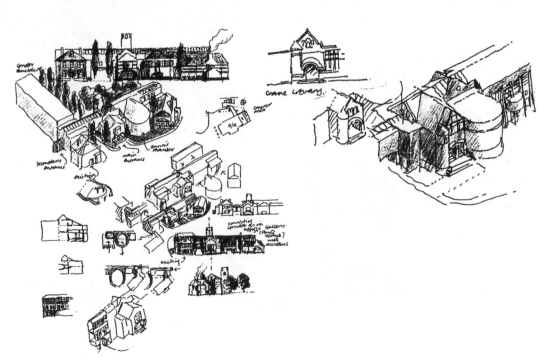

21.1 Richard Reid's drawings of Epping High Street provide the context for the design of his town hall. The dictates of function are moderated by a concern for the historic fabric of the town. These sketches show how place and programme are reconciled.

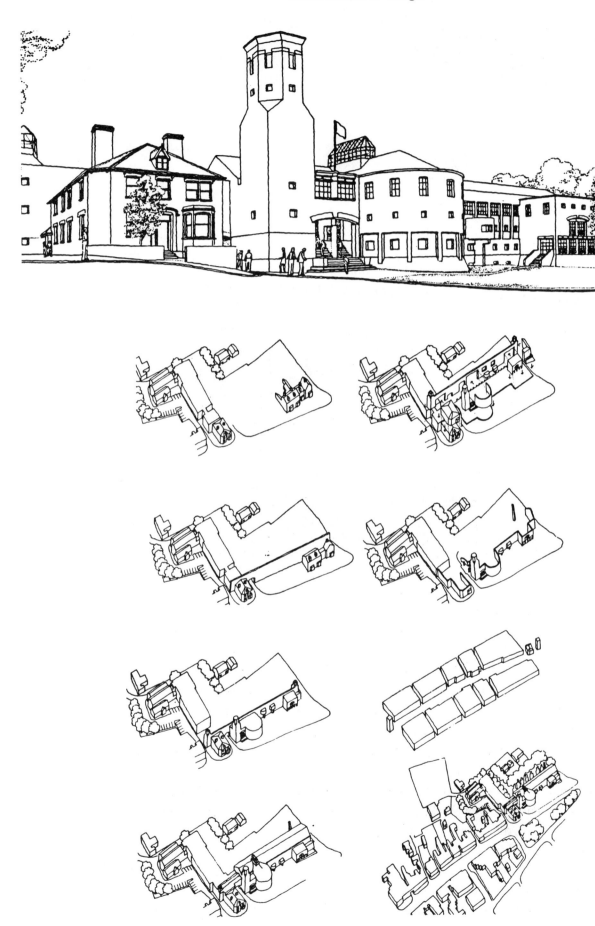

21.1 Continued

only provides a rich repertoire of details and forms from which to seek inspiration, but teaches something of the significance of particular places and their functions. To draw an area of 18th-century London, for instance, is to realize how important buildings and squares are to each other – to understand that a designer must consider both the buildings and the space they occupy. Similarly, sketches of Los Angeles show how central the road and parking lot are to modern civic design. If you were to sketch in parts of Paris or New York, you may also discover the urban significance of corner sites – not just as a place for architectural display, but as a location for prime real estate.

The process of drawing is, therefore, crucial to understanding the significance of architectural 'events' in the urban scene. Gateways may be special buildings but their real value to you as a designer is to help you establish the relative importance of such structures within the hierarchy of the city. Designers have responsibilities towards the town as well as their clients: addressing questions of legibility, order, hierarchy and continuity are part of the architect and urban designer's wider duties.

By sketching you will begin to understand the visual structure of an area, and the various details which collectively make up cityscape or landscape. Places are assemblies of parts held together by an organizing principle. The latter may be simple, such as an urban grid of streets or a network of docks, or complex, such as an inner-city neigh-

21.2 This sequence of a photograph and sketches showing urban changes demonstrate how flexible the graphic medium is. In this case Hawksmoor's church at St Anne's Limehouse in London Docklands is opened to view by removing the clutter of recent buildings in Commercial Road.

bourhood made up of fragmented parts. Landscapes, although superficially beautiful, are often composed of irregular or dislocated elements. It is analysis through the sketchbook, rather than through words, that can best unravel these complexities.

Designing from the basis of a sharpened visual perception is of obvious benefit to you, your client and to the environment. If your task is relatively simple, such as designing a new house, then it is a straightforward undertaking to sketch the houses in the neighbourhood, recording their basic shapes and window, door, roof and wall details. The cataloguing of parts and general arrangements make a good starting point for the design of the new house. Your ambitions as a designer may go further than blindly repeating the pattern round about, but a clever architect will reinterpret the old forms, not invent completely new ones. Should you decide to place a glass box in a neighbourhood of Arts and Crafts houses, then it is hardly surprising that the planning authority will take a dislike to your design.

The form and details of what you have drawn are important, but so is their significance. A particular assembly of glass and steel on an office block may prove useful in the design of objects unrelated to architecture, such as in furniture or product design. The way the juxtaposition of materials is handled can, therefore, have a universal application. Similarly, an aircraft wing may provide clues as to how a building could be put together – the moving parts giving hints, for instance, as to how flexible solar screening could operate. When drawing, one should be asking questions about the subject, discovering the essence rather than merely recording the surface forms. It is often the underlying principles, more than the details, which prove a source of inspiration in design.

It is obvious that the way we draw influences how we think about places and buildings, and hence plays a significant part in how we might approach design. The use of perspective drawing, axonometric, figure-ground or shadow-enhanced image shapes our perception of the subject. The current fashionable interest in figure-ground representation has discouraged the deconstructed distortions of many designers. Five hundred years ago the discovery of geometric perspective led to a similar interest in spatial patterns, vistas and terminations.

If drawing sharpens our visual awareness, the method of representation directly influences how we view the world. To move from sketchbook exploration to design requires the intermediary of a drawing. Many graphic techniques are available, from simple plan, section and elevation to more elaborate methods of three-dimensional representation. Whichever method is chosen, it is important to follow the established rules, rather than make up new conventions as you go along. Like writing or mathematics, the rules are well understood and relatively inviolable. The grammar of drawing, its syntax and composition are important matters, whether you be graphic illustrator or designer.

The shift in emphasis from sketchbook studies to questions of design requires an appreciation of some simple theories of architecture. Like all patterns formed by the interrelationship of objects and space, the architecture of buildings and cities can be understood from various perspectives. One can view the subject in terms of space, surface, structure or decoration. Architecture as space has long captivated designers who have contrived to carve complex spatial effects out of the solid mass of buildings or even whole cities. Baroque churches and many modern office buildings enhanced with atria manipulate architectural space to dramatic effect. Even in relatively small rooms space can be moulded and modified to excite the senses.

Architecture as plane or surface is the converse of architecture as space, though obviously both cannot be considered in isolation. Here the interest is in design of the surfaces which define the spaces, both inside and out. As the surfaces are what we see, they have long fascinated the topographical artist, for it is they that provide clues to the function and significance of a building. Focusing on the surfaces allows the designer to exploit modelling, hierarchy of form, colour and

21.3 *Another sequence of a photograph and sketches remodels Great Western Road in Glasgow by removing the traffic and planting trees. Notice how the first drawing begins to edit out the unnecessary information of the photograph.*

21.4 *A more ambitious change is described by way of sketches at the Gorbals in Glasgow. Here Alexander Thomson's church is freed of the visual competition of tower blocks and given a square at the front.*

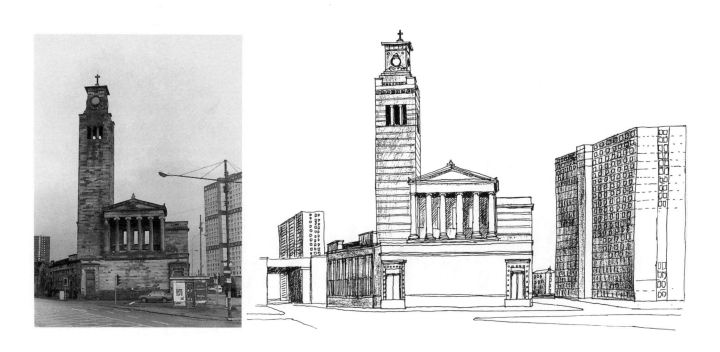

texture in order to transmit to the observer the 'meaning' of a building.

Architecture as structure is another readily understood classification. It derives great legitimacy from modernist functional theory which requires the honest expression of the means of supporting a building. To take an example from history, Gothic cathedrals were as concerned with structional expression as with the moulding of space. The visible display of a building's structure can greatly influence one's perception of both its interior and exterior.

Architecture as decoration concerns itself with applied embellishment. The task of the designer is to provide enough decoration to allow people to understand and enjoy the building. Decorative detail can relate the building to its surroundings or

function by adopting a familiar code of expression, or allow advertising in some form or another. Decoration provides a cheap and ready means of instilling symbolism for commercial, civic or private reasons.

These four key interests should be integrated in a design. The integrity or appropriateness of a design – whether it be for a chair, building or city – should be generated by weighing the demands of functional arrangement against these principal means of expression. The designer has the task of striking the balance and relating it to other points mentioned earlier, such as the physical or historical context. Sometimes the clue to how the balance should be struck derives from precedent (churches are often concerned with space and symbolism, while office buildings focus upon structure and

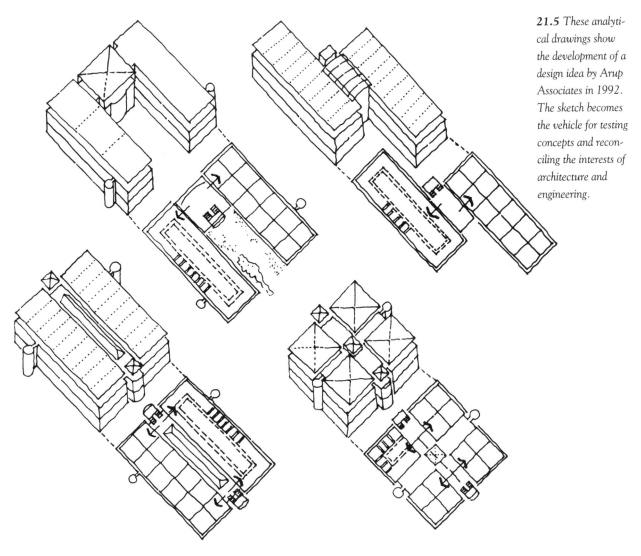

21.5 These analytical drawings show the development of a design idea by Arup Associates in 1992. The sketch becomes the vehicle for testing concepts and reconciling the interests of architecture and engineering.

21.6 In these sketches (of 1992) Arup Associates seek to establish the development framework for a business park. The sketches try to integrate the needs of urban, landscape and engineering design.

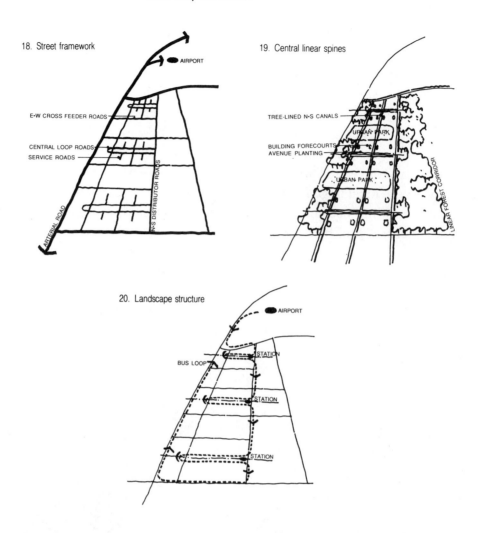

18. Street framework

19. Central linear spines

20. Landscape structure

surface) or the dictates of context. Whether as a student of architecture, a professional involved in the construction industry, or as an interested lay person, a visual awareness sharpened by use of the sketchbook leads quite naturally to a sensitivity towards design.

Many designers employ the freehand drawing to help develop their ideas. A completed design proposal does not happen all at once; rather it grows from a series of early sketches and abstract probings. The sketch plan or section allows the architect to grasp the complexity of the subject and develop particular strands. The methods employed in reaching an understanding of an existing building or place are much the same as those used to develop a design proposal. Such drawings have the prime objective of explaining to the architect aspects of the design. A series of sketch drawings are normally prepared, each representing a layer of

development or an aspect of the design. They can be used in three important ways:

- to relate new design proposals to the existing structure of site and buildings;
- to communicate the broad design strategy to others involved in the creative process;
- to analyse and explain aspects of the design to oneself.

Mention has already been made of how Charles Rennie Mackintosh and Richard Reid use the freehand drawing as part of the creative act. For many architects and engineers the sketch is an essential starting point for any design proposal. The investigation of options and the development of particular avenues of thought are best achieved through the medium of the freehand sketch. There comes a time when a more critical and analytical approach

21.7 *This sketch by Ted Cullinan is based upon a master-class in urban design held in Glasgow in 1992. Cullinan's 'dot' drawing proposes a new gateway building near Cathedral Square.*

21.8 *The same masterclass (see figure 21.7) led to the development of this proposal for decking over the M8 motorway near Glasgow's Mitchell Library. The drawing by architect Terry Pawson uses free graphics to capture the spirit rather than details of the proposal.*

is needed, and here formal perspective drawings or computer simulation can be useful. But at the conceptual stage, when designs are still fluid and where a number of options need to be explored quickly, the sketch can be invaluable. At this point the designer will be relating the plan and form of the proposed building to such matters as function; considering how to link patterns of circulation to the section; and having initial thoughts about structure and servicing. Depending upon the project in hand, the designer will probably be grappling with questions of site layout, landscaping and shelter. These and many other issues lend themselves to the freehand sketch, not as a means of recording a final decision, but as a method of weighing up options from the point of view of design and the organization of form and space.

For the artist to become comfortable with using drawing as a creative tool, the sketchbook must be employed as a means of recording and analysing existing buildings. The sense of a 'sketchbook culture' needs to underpin the creative design process.

Arup Associates, whose designs have received many recent awards, operate in much this fashion. Here design proposals are explored around the central focus of the sketch. The concept for the whole building, and its various parts, is explained to mixed teams of architects and engineers using the sketch of a plan, section or detail as the starting point for debate. The lack of distinction in Arup Associates office between architects and engineers has resulted in a climate where most designers, irrespective of their backgrounds, have become skilful communicators through the medium of the freehand sketch.

21.10 *Richard Reid's sketch of his housing proposal for Finland Quay in London Docklands uses boats and people to give scale and interest to the public spaces.*

Further reading

Bacon, E. (1967) *The Design of Cities*. Thames and Hudson, London.

Bentley, I., Alcock, A., Murrain, P., McGlynn, S. and Smith, G. (1985) *Responsive Environments: A Manual for Designers*. Architectural Press, London.

Broadbent, G. (1990) *Emerging Concepts in Urban Space Design*. Van Nostrand Reinhold (International), London and New York.

Cullen, G. (1961) *The Concise Townscape*. Architectural Press, London.

Giedion, S. (1941) *Space, Time and Architecture*, 1954 edn. Harvard University Press.

HRH, the Prince of Wales (1989) *A Vision for Britain: A Personal View of Architecture*. Doubleday, London.

Hogarth, P. (1973) *Drawing Architecture: A Creative Approach*. Pitman, London.

Lynch, K. (1960) *The Image of the City*. MIT Press, Cambridge and London.

Rossi, A. (1982) *The Architecture of the City*. MIT Press, Cambridge and London.

Index